# HARRY THODE

## Scientist and Builder
## at McMaster University

*by*

Manuel Zack, Lawrence Martin & Alvin A. Lee

mcmaster university press

Published in 2003 by McMaster University Press
Printed and Bound in Canada

For further information or to order additional copies contact:
Office of the Vice-President, University Advancement
McMaster University
1280 Main Street West
Hamilton, Ontario, Canada  L8S 4K1
(905) 525-9140   www.mcmaster.ca


National Library of Canada Cataloguing in Publication Data


Zack, Manuel, 1917-1999
  Harry Thode : scientist and builder at McMaster University / by Manuel Zack,
  Lawrence Martin & Alvin A. Lee.


Includes bibliographical references.
ISBN 1-894088-38-7 (bound).--ISBN 1-894088-40-9 (pbk.)


1. Thode, Henry George, 1910-1997.
2. College presidents--Ontario--Hamilton--Biography.
3. McMaster University--Biography.
I. Martin, Lawrence, 1947-  II. Lee, Alvin A., 1930-  III. Title.

LE3.M317T46 2003      378.713'52'092        C2003-901359-6

For SADIE THODE
*With Respect and Gratitude*

# Contents

# Foreword

Harry Thode was a man of vision. He was an outstanding scholar, an exceptional educator, and a world-renowned scientist. As an administrator, he demonstrated a gift for identifying talented people, trusting them with responsibility and empowering them to carry through. He was a creative, informed risk-taker whose legacy can be felt throughout the McMaster campus to this day.

Thode served as McMaster President from 1961 to 1972, and, during those 11 years, he ushered the university into a new era. He was instrumental in the development of McMaster's first graduate programs, and he played a prominent role in the creation of the Faculty of Engineering and the Faculty of Health Sciences. His presidency at McMaster saw a construction boom that included the Nuclear Reactor (the first on a university campus in the British Commonwealth), the new Arts complex, and the Health Sciences Centre. As University President, he set the stage for the recruitment of the outstanding visionaries who created the McMaster Medical School. Under his guidance, they pioneered the philosophy of problem-based learning and interdisciplinary collaboration that has proven to be one of McMaster's most distinguishing characteristics.

McMaster University was a very different place from the university of today when Harry Thode first arrived in 1939. The world was two weeks away from the outbreak of the Second World War. Within three years of his arrival at McMaster, the young associate professor of chemistry had earned such recognition as a scientist that the Canadian Government asked for his assistance. Harry Thode's wartime research played a significant role in the development of nuclear science and helped put McMaster on the map as an institution that nourishes outstanding researchers.

A distinguished researcher in nuclear science and geochemistry and one of the university's most important builders, Harry Thode is the man who defined the modern day McMaster. His ideals continue to inspire us. His belief in McMaster and his unwavering commitment to our university serve as treasured memories to everyone who had the honour to know him.

**Peter George**
*President and Vice-Chancellor*
*McMaster University*

# Preface and Acknowledgments

It is now 63 and a half years since Harry Thode came to McMaster, in the fall of 1939, and began his career as a research scientist and administrator. Probably no one since then has had a comparable shaping impact on the development of the university. Thode's two main professional ambitions were to excel individually as a physical scientist, in the fields of geochemistry and nuclear chemistry, and, more publicly, to transform McMaster University into a major research centre, to make it a place where students learned from professors who were active in research. Thode undoubtedly succeeded in the first of these ambitions. He had major successes in the second, especially but not only during his administrative years. Both sets of accomplishments are recorded in the pages that follow.

In 1939, McMaster was a respected but relatively modest institution, with its major purpose the teaching of undergraduate students in arts, science, and theology. To be sure, its professoriate included isolated examples of genuine research and scholarship, individuals who were recognized nationally and in some cases internationally, but these few scholars were more a matter of individual talent and drive than of institutional intention. It was Thode, more than anyone else, who changed the university's character for the foreseeable future. For a long time now, most of the approximately 1000 McMaster faculty members, located in six strong faculties, have been engaged in research and scholarship that both informs their educational work and helps extend the frontiers of their disciplines. Unfortunately there was a major and relentless weakening of public support for Ontario's universities in the latter part of Thode's life (he died in 1997, 25 years after leaving the presidency), with an impact on McMaster that he observed with growing dismay. Although this was a period in which other individuals had the administrative responsibilities, the university still in important ways was and is his creation. Nationally and internationally it is an important centre of scholarship and research.

The academic structure and governance of the university are far from anything envisaged by Thode, back in the relatively oligarchic days of his early career. The academic diversity and complexity of McMaster are dramatically different from his initial vision of what they should be. For example, for years now, many students and researchers have opted for the life sciences and the professions rather than the physical sciences, which were more popular in Thode's time and were central to his own research interests. There has been an extensive complication and diversification of the work of the medical and health science professions. The explosion of knowledge and intellectual achievement in a wide range of arts disciplines at McMaster is not something that ever had a large place in Thode's plans. These changes nonetheless have been major characteristics of the university for more than thirty years. As in most other universities but with its own institutional emphases, two realities are studied intensively at McMaster: the actual physical and natural world, by scientists, and the realities of human culture, by humanists and social scientists. Researchers in the professional schools and faculties regularly test their knowledge of science and of human culture in the light of the applied needs and pressures of their particular professions. In spite of all these divergences from Thode's initial vision, it is a historical fact that he did more than anyone else to create on this campus the research climate that still characterizes McMaster. It is he who established the base that made possible here in the second half of the 20th century a host of important, even major, research achievements, and the high-level educational experiences that happen only in such places.

This book is essentially a chronicle, at times an annalistic one, of Thode's career as a scientist and university administrator. It records the major events and achievements of Thode the university man. It does not delve deeply into the psychology, sociology, or history that would be relevant to a full telling of the story of the life of Harry Thode. In other words, this book is not a biography in an extended, in-depth sense of the word. There are of course many such notable recent biographical studies in our libraries, including those written by McMaster professors. For that kind of more sustained and ambitious work, as, for example, Alan Walker's three-volume biography of Franz Liszt, years or decades of careful research, hard analysis, and imaginative thought enable the biographer plausibly to claim detailed knowledge of the individual being presented. That kind of scholarship normally includes attempts to get to the inner motivations of the subject, as well as to the more visible ones. It involves a detailed account of the individual's family and friends and, when appropriate, of his or her social and historical dimensions. The best examples of such studies demonstrate as well a heightened awareness of the cultural determinants that helped make the particular individual what he or she was.

Our goals are more modest, partly out of respect for Harry Thode who, for all his public work, was a deeply private man not prone to talk a lot about himself, as distinct from his research, and partly also out of respect for the privacy of Mrs. Sadie Thode, their three sons John, Patrick, and Richard, and their families. There are glimpses of these individuals in the following pages, especially of Sadie Thode. She and her family have been extraordinarily helpful and patient as this book slowly took shape. Still, we know that to do anything like justice to any or all of them as important human beings, in a true biography of Harry Thode, would entail research and inquiry well beyond the scope of this chronicle.

Similarly, there is another story which, with due research and time, could be told about Thode as a man with involvements in the business world. That particular narrative would deal with the important fact that business people have been part of the Thode family for four or five generations, and still are, in the person of Harry and Sadie's son Patrick. But that body of material too, except in the occasional references made to Thode's business interests as they touched on his work at McMaster, would take this book beyond its purpose.

Readers of the pages that follow will detect several voices: those of numerous individuals who were interviewed and those of the three authors. Initially and with extraordinary enthusiasm and dedication, Manny Zack, who was Thode's executive assistant during his presidency, did a mass of sleuthing, interviewing of individuals (including Thode himself), and recording of important materials, and so put in place much of the groundwork and some of the text of this book. But Zack's untimely death terminated that part of the project. The chronologically second major voice in the preparation is that of Lawrence Martin, a McMaster graduate and well known journalist (and biographer of Jean Chrétien and Lucien Bouchard), who, under commission, conducted further research and interviews, and wrote much of the present text. John Thode has been the major source for family background. His brother Patrick has helped generously with numerous facts, especially those about his father's life beyond the university. He also provided overall help in shaping the narrative of the book. Arthur Bourns, with assistance from several colleagues, has made sure that the account of Thode's work as scientist is accurately told. In addition, his memory of Thode and many of the administrative developments they lived through together has been invaluable. Numerous other voices are heard in this chronicle, often in the form of direct quotation but sometimes less directly. We gratefully acknowledge the help of all of those who have contributed. Appendices Two to Four are reprinted with permission, respectively, from Professor B.A.W. Jackson, The Royal Society (London), and the Geological Society of America.

At the request of President Peter George, Roger Trull for the last three years has chaired a working group comprised of Arthur Bourns, Patrick Thode, Richard Tomlinson, and myself, to ensure that this project is brought to completion. Caroline Gordon and Dylan Bailey in Roger's office and Julia Thomson in the Office of Public Relations have provided important help. Richard Tomlinson, Thode's long-time colleague and friend, has generously funded the project. I have gone over the text in detail and made a host of changes, many of them to do with small but not unimporant matters, but some more substantive, to help ensure that this is an accurate, balanced, and fairly literate account of the work of Harry Thode and its large impact on McMaster University.

**Alvin A. Lee**
*President Emeritus, McMaster University*

# Chapter One

# Growing up in Saskatchewan

Henry G. Thode was the second son of Charles Thode who, as the century turned, had come to Saskatchewan, then called Assiniboia, from the rich farm country of Iowa. Charles took out a homestead of 160 acres south of Saskatoon. It cost him ten dollars, which was about the going rate in the western territories at the time. The Thode homestead lay at the top of an elevation, looking down over the village of Dundurn, which was settled by Scottish ranchers. The Thodes were situated east of the town and the river.

Young Harry's was a life that seemed blessed from the beginning. He grew up in a comfortable, relatively secure, and devoted family, whose circumstances allowed him to pursue his curiosity and develop his academic gifts. His father, Charles, who was of Germanic ancestry, was a hard-working farmer, always alert to the possibilities of improvement. Having studied agricultural science for two years at the University of South Dakota, the elder Thode sought out the newest fertilizers, the newest tools, the newest machinery, and the newest methods to keep himself ahead of his more complacent peers. He bought and sold land and used his profits to expand into other businesses connected to farming.

On his father's side, Charles Thode came from two generations of farmers who had settled in Wisconsin and Iowa. They had originally emigrated from Schleswig-Holstein near the present-day border of Germany and Denmark, hoping to avoid military service and lured by the new opportunities for farmers in America's welcoming expanse. For his parents and grandparents, Harry would recall, with an appreciation for their solid virtues and simple outlook, "the land was a saint. You could make a living off the land, you could grow food, there was always a market for food."

On Harry's mother's side were the Jacobys, who originated in the Brandenburg region of Prussia. Unlike the Thodes, the Jacobys were business

1

*Thode homestead near Dundurn, Saskatchewan where Harry Thode was born in 1910*

people, accountants and shoemakers, but they too made their way to America. Harry's mother, the vivacious Zelma Ann Jacoby, born in 1886 in the town of Windom, Minnesota, was one of ten children. In 1902, immediately following the death of her father, she and her family boarded the Sioux Railway for Assiniboia. Most of the space on the train was given over to livestock and Zelma remembered it as a slow trip, with many stops on the way during which she and other passengers were called upon to take the animals into the fields to feed. The Jacobys' destination happened to be Dundurn, where Zelma's two older brothers had opened a general store. Into that store one day in 1907 came Charlie Thode. There to buy a hammer, he ended up with a wife. He and Zelma were married the same year. They had their first boy, the fair-haired Eckart, a year later. Harry, christened Henry George, followed after two years; then came Margaret, William, and John. September was always a busy month, with four out of five of the Thode children celebrating their birthdays.

Harry attended kindergarten in the village for a few months before the family moved to Saskatoon. Graced by the beauty of the curving Saskatchewan River, Saskatoon was an attractive small city that was experiencing rapid growth with the arrival of the transcontinental Canadian Pacific Railway. Six- and seven-storey buildings—skyscrapers, the locals called them—were starting to rise from the city centre. Charlie Thode was prosperous enough to purchase a three-storey stucco and wood home on the second wealthiest street in town. Located at 832 University Drive, the house had a heated garage, two bathrooms, two fireplaces, and an unheated porch off the master bedroom. The Thodes also enjoyed the twin luxuries of a maid and a car (Zelma broke her arm while cranking the family's first Ford).

While they enjoyed a comfortable lifestyle, the Thodes were not a profligate or ostentatious family. Charles stuck to business most of the time, leading by example, the boys recalled, while Zelma ran the house and the social calendar. Resilient and outgoing, she liked everyone and expected everyone to like her back. As a young teen in Minnesota, she had fallen from a ladder and broken her nose. No doctors were around to fix it. "One had to go as far as New York. Nothing was done for my nose except to open one nostril. I was teased a good deal by children. With a child's face and a large nose, it was very conspicuous and I had many battles over it." Though her features were irregular, Zelma's wavy blonde hair, vivacity, and good eye for presentation gave her a distinctive charm. As a schoolgirl, she had learned the importance of good behaviour. She and her boyfriend once got caught sledding down a forbidden hill. When a policeman caught the young pair, he fined them five dollars. "This was a fortune for me," Zelma recalled, "So my friend paid my fine and I paid him back in nickels and dimes. I learned it always pays to obey the law."

Harry appeared to inherit his father's focus and his mother's liveliness. As a young student at Victoria Public School, he was friendly, popular, and adventuresome, even mischievous. A clever student, he took grades three and four in one year and did the same for grades seven and eight. On his way home from school he often stopped by his grandmother's house to receive tutoring from his Aunt Frieda. Frieda had been a schoolteacher and, as he put it, "she knew all the tricks of the trade." Harry's sister Margaret, who was four years younger, does not recall him being a particularly hard-working student; knowledge just came to him naturally. His older brother Eckart, who missed some schooling due to illness, was not pleased at the younger Harry skipping grades and catching up to him, and the two had many brotherly battles in their early years. At school, an English teacher once asked Harry to comment on the quality of one of Eckart's compositions. Harry could not help giving his brother's paper a rough review, suggesting it was short on originality. He later felt guilty about saying something against one of his own in public. Although their relationship went through some rocky patches when they were children, the two got along much better in later years.

For the Thode parents, one of the attractions of moving to Saskatoon was its well-regarded school system. While living in the city, Charlie continued to run his farms in Dundurn and to maintain his country home. During the summers Harry got up early in the mornings to feed, brush, harness, and drive his father's stable of horses, before they were replaced by tractors. The adventuresome boy was always up to something. Once he was towed off into the fields by runaway horses. Another time he was caught smoking cigarettes behind the barn.

When the family moved to Saskatoon, it became possible for the children to have the best of both worlds. Harry's mother later recalled that the move made available to them "the best educational system in the West at the time and the benefit of farm life in the summer." They learned the intricacies of the farm business. Their father would teach them the facts of life on the farm and how to make a garden. He was excited about gardening and making things grow, and he wanted his children to be excited.

The family went on several trips. Especially memorable for Harry was a visit to Yellowstone National Park, where he was fascinated by the geysers. Perhaps this experience contributed to his life-long interest in geology. Much of his later isotope research was related to the geological history of the earth and of the solar system. His sons recall that he often showed them fossils and glacial grooves in the exposed limestone at his farm on Lake Erie. When he became interested in a rock formation, he would often take samples and measure their sulphur isotope ratios which provided clues to their geological history.

Zelma found it easier to raise Harry and the other boys on the farm than in the city. She thought it was more wholesome and offered fewer distractions to undermine family unity than the "big city." While growing up, he and the other children all had their assigned tasks. One of their jobs was to kill off the gophers that were getting at the grain. The Thode boys treated the wheat with a little syrup and a generous amount of strychnine. "This was wholesale murder but it cut down on the loss of grain," recalls Harry's mother. The gophers would find rows of newly drilled grain before it came up or germinated. The boys used to like snaring and shooting them; the government gave them two cents a tail.

Always looking for an edge on the competition, Charlie Thode had one of the first tractors in Saskatchewan. It was manufactured in his native Iowa and he went there for a few weeks to learn how to operate and repair it, before having it sent up north. As well as his several farming enterprises, he tried his hand at a variety of businesses. He had a considerable interest in a lumber operation in northeastern Saskatchewan, was part owner of a packing plant that later went bankrupt, and he joined with another investor in establishing the Whitaker Wholesale Grocery House. Charlie drove his farm employees hard but took care of the good workers, looking after their welfare in hard times, helping them finance the building of their own farms, and seeing to it that they had diversions from the daily grind. He organized track and field meets in the summers and bonspiels in the winters.

Though young Harry took part in high school football, sports did not appeal to him as much as they did to many other teenagers. He loved swimming and later became a member of the water polo team at university. His mother taught him golf and did not hesitate to fetch him from school for the odd afternoon round, when he had moved on to secondary school at Nutana Collegiate. His father was an avid curler and taught Harry that staple sport of western Canada. The memory of his excitement in watching his father at the bonspiels was something that stayed with Harry forever. Later in life, he would reflect on how curling was "quite a scientific game," and once went into great detail about the game for an interviewer from eastern Canada.There was a curling rink in Dundurn and his father belonged to the Saskatoon curling rink as well and went to bonspiels in Regina, Edmonton, and Winnipeg. Young Harry was proud that his dad was the skip, "the man who was leading the team and plotting the strategy, telling them where to throw their rocks and how much weight to put on them." Harry would relay the curling exploits of his father to his friends in much the same way as a boy whose father was in the big leagues of hockey.

The elder Thodes spoke a fair bit of German and would occasionally use it around the house when they did not want their children to know what they were talking about. But they did not teach the children the language.

Harry's generally happy childhood was interrupted by one tragic episode. His youngest brother, John, died at the age of two, when Harry was 15. "It was a very sudden thing," recalls sister Margaret. "He was out at the farm with mother. It was the spring and she had gone down to stay with Dad for a few days while the rest of us remained in the city. The doctor there said it was only the flu and not to worry about him. But Johnnie woke up in the night and mother noticed he was delirious. They rushed him to hospital in Saskatoon, but he lived only a day or two."

Harry was impressed by the quality of his teachers at Nutana Collegiate, where he studied Latin, French, English, history, physics, chemistry, and mathematics. But the enthusiasm generated by a chemistry teacher, Mr. Wilson, instilled in him a greater interest in science than in the other subjects. This exceptional teacher, he recalled, was able "to capture our imagination by performing exciting experiments. This, no doubt, influenced my career choice." While friendly and outgoing, Harry also had a competitive streak; he relished the rivalry he had with the other students who excelled in chemistry and math, like his great friend Bob Atkinson, a top student who became a medical doctor. Sadly, Bob Atkinson died of polio shortly after graduation. The senior Thode had hopes that Eckart or Harry would follow him into the farming business, but he did not pressure them, and neither of them was inclined in that direction. As already noted, the third son, William (Bill), did become a farmer. Harry, his curiosity fired by Mr. Wilson's experiments, was leaning toward a career in chemistry.

Having done four of the earlier grades in two years, Harry was ready to enter university at 16, in 1926. The University of Saskatchewan at Saskatoon had been established in 1907 with Walter Murray, a philosophy professor from the Maritimes, as its first president. The institution was gaining a strong reputation for applied scientific research in agriculture and other fields. Notable professors had been hired to seek solutions to practical problems, such as the red rust fungus that was destroying the wheat harvests. When it was decided that the Saskatchewan River needed a bridge, C.J. Mackenzie, who had been a classmate at Harvard of C.D. Howe, was appointed dean of engineering. He soon had his students helping develop plans for a reinforced concrete bridge, one of the first of its type.

The chemistry department eventually produced an alkaline-resistant cement that resisted crumbling under the effects of calcium sulphate. The fresh, optimistic environment of the fledgling university was an ideal complement to Harry's keen scientific curiosity. That it was science, not the arts, that was his destiny became evident early in his university career. He failed his first-year compulsory English course and had to take a supplemental exam. Thode simply could not, or would not, wrap his mind around the likes of Chaucer or Shakespeare or Thackeray. He was never a keen reader of novels or non-scientific books. His sister Margaret recalls, "He didn't like that kind of work. He always showed more interest in the sciences. I preferred English and economics and things like that. I liked to read but he wasn't a reader that way."

Eckart and Harry took many of the same courses at university, and friends called them, respectively, Big Todey and Little Todey. Eventually, they parted academic paths, with Eckart concentrating on accounting. Competition between the brothers was not limited to the classroom. At a dance they both attended, Harry and his taller, blonder, and more handsome brother both became intrigued by the same girl, Sadie Patrick. A friend introduced the petite Sadie to Harry, who was sporting a regular suit, and to Eckart, who was resplendent in a tux. She danced with both, and was amused when, in the days before the next dance, she received phone calls from both brothers, asking her to accompany them. The first call was from Harry, so Eckart lost out. In the years ahead, Sadie Thode would often be given to wonder what might have happened if the calls had come in reverse order. She and Harry got on well, though according to Margaret the intrigue was not limited to the two brothers. Sadie had a sister, Pat, to whom Harry was initially attracted. Pat was a livewire and had a lot of boyfriends, but "eventually Harry liked Sadie better," Margaret recalls. If there was competition from her sister, Sadie was oblivious to it.

Sadie appeared intent on setting her own career path. At home in Yorkton, her entry into school had been delayed until age seven because the grade one class was too crowded. Disappointment led to determination, and she set about learning to read at home. At university, she studied dietetics and home economics, which required courses in chemistry and physics. Third-year student Harry Thode had been made a laboratory assistant, and Sadie was one of his first-year students. Chemistry never caught her interest in the same way that it had Harry. She was more inclined to the arts.

The couple went skating, dancing, and to the movies, and they enjoyed listening to music on the Thodes' top-quality record player. Sadie soon became quite a favourite among Harry's family. She remembers fondly the time Harry's visiting grandfather came to say goodnight to her and Harry in the living room. On his way out he turned and said, "I hope you will be happy for many years." Sadie was touched by these simple words.

Sadie could see that Harry Thode was a pragmatic man who would be a successful scientist, but she worried that he did not share her cultural interests or her more romantic view of life. She knew she did not share his love of farm life, which she found harsh and uncomfortable. She came from Yorkton, about 225 miles of dirt road from Saskatoon, and she returned there for the long summers, to work as a clerk and earn tuition money.

7

Harry drove the twelve hours there and back to see her once or twice each summer, and she noticed he was always in a hurry to get back to the farm.

While they were in university, Charlie rented for Harry and Eckart a big farm plot to operate and manage themselves, telling them that, if they were to have money for university, they had to earn it. The brothers lived in a store-house which stocked machinery at one end and grain at the other. They bunked down in the corner of the machine shed at night. Sister Margaret sometimes brought her cat down to kill the mice and cooked the odd meal. "It was just one large room and they slept in there; it was really very primitive. I hated it when I had to go down there," she says. The only day of leisure was Sunday, when they would go down to Proctor's Lake for a swim.

Harry finished his undergraduate degree in good standing but his grades were not high enough to win any awards. Bursaries from the National Research Council in Ottawa went to other students, as did a scholarship to McGill University. In the case of the latter, Harry was angry that the head of the chemistry department had shown favouritism to one of his personal researchers. He was not one to brood, however: "Once something like that happened, he just forgot about it and went on," says Sadie.

Harry decided to stay in Saskatoon to pursue his master's degree and his relationship with Sadie. His academic supervisor was Dr. A.C. Grubb, a physical chemist educated at Purdue University and the University of Chicago. When Grubb suffered a lengthy illness, Harry was called in to help teach his undergraduate courses, thus gaining valuable classroom experience. Thode's master's research project into the properties of ozone seemed very theoretical at the time. To make ozone he passed oxygen through a corona discharge tube that contained a high-voltage wire. "I was measuring the ozone concentration at the other end of the tube," recalled Thode, "and as long as there was a steady state, the amount of ozone concentration was the same hour after hour. As soon as you put some chemical in there and the ozone started decomposing faster and faster, then you'd get less and less. Today we know that the fluorocarbons that go up into the upper atmosphere cause the rapid decay of the ozone layer."

Owing to his father's business acumen, the Thode family was protected from the worst effects of the Depression that devastated the Prairies. Charlie Thode was able to keep most of his farming business going near Dundurn, which, during the dustbowl days, was not as hot and dry as southern Saskatchewan. His wholesale grocery business went bankrupt, but he was still making enough money to allow his sons and daughters to continue their educations. But times were rough for the community as a whole: "I remember that they came to Dad during the Depression and said if he didn't pay his taxes they'd have to close the school," recalls Margaret. "I know a teacher who wanted to quit because she got paid with five cows and she couldn't live on that."

On finishing his master's thesis, Thode had to decide whether to remain in Canada to do his doctorate, to head overseas to Britain or Germany, or to go south to the United States. In his home country, his choices in chemistry were limited to McGill and the University of Toronto. At both schools the program directors were pursuing areas that did not coincide with his interests. Germany was the leader in chemistry research and Thode inquired of the head of his department whether he should pursue that option. He was advised against it, which was fortunate given Germany's drift at the time into fascism followed by war-mongering. A Rhodes scholarship to Oxford would have delighted Harry but he did not meet the qualifications. By process of elimination, then, the United States appeared to offer the best opportunities. Two organic chemists whom he admired in his own department had received their doctorates from the University of Chicago under reputed scientist Julius Steiglitz. They and others encouraged him to apply, in 1932, for a scholarship and for admission to Chicago's doctoral program.

*Thode homestead as it looked in the 1960s under the ownership of Harry Thode's brother Bill Thode*

*Harry Thode (right) with (left to right) brothers Eckart and Bill and sister Margaret (c. 1919)*

*Harry Thode (right) with (left to right) brother Eckart, mother Zelma (age 95), brother Bill, and sister Margaret (1981)*

*Harry Thode with his father, Charles Herman Thode (age 92), and three of Harry's grandchildren at his Lynden, Ontario farm (1973)*

# Chapter Two

## Doctoral Work in Chicago, Teaching in Pittsburgh, Postdoctoral Work at Columbia, 1932-1938

Thode won acceptance to the University of Chicago's doctoral program, but did not hear back about the scholarship. He would have to rely on his father for more funds. While not in the financially robust state he had been before the economic downturn, Charles Thode could still afford to send his son away to the prestigious university. Before Harry left to take up his new life, his father insisted that he stay to bring in the harvest. Harry was bitter for days: "I remember him being so upset," Margaret recalls.

While his father encouraged higher education, he also wanted to instil the value of farming into his scholarly son. Harry's technical talk on research in pure chemistry, and on ozone layers and corona discharge tubes, did not mean much to his parents. But the young man knew that the prospects for making a good living in farming were slim to nil during the Depression. There were no prices for the crops. People were leaving the farms because it was all work and no pay. The rich topsoil was disappearing in the dust storms. "I remember when I wrote my exams in the drill hall in 1932," says Sadie. "You had to stop about every two minutes to blow the dust off your paper. You could hardly breathe, never mind farm." Had conditions been more favourable in the 1930s, according to Sadie, Harry might have become a farmer, and Canada might have lost one of its finest science researchers and educators.

Harry talked to Sadie about her joining him in the Windy City, but, because she had no money and debts from her schooling to pay off, she chose, instead to move to Toronto to take a course in hospital dietetics at the Hospital for Sick Children. The young couple were not sure that they would get back together again. They agreed to begin dating others.

On arrival in Chicago by train, the twenty-two-year-old, wide-eyed prairie boy was immediately struck by the towering buildings, landscaped outer drive, broad windswept streets, and elevated transit system. Soup kitchens and the legions of the unemployed and the bankrupt were little in evidence on the elite university campus or in the more well-to-do areas in which Harry travelled. Preparations were in full force for the 1933 World's Fair, for which an island was being built in Lake Michigan.

Thode moved into an apartment with his cousin, Neil Jacoby, who had been born and raised in Dundurn and was now studying economics at the university. The city had a reputation for gangsterism—Al Capone's St. Valentine's Day massacre had occurred there in 1929—and Thode, while not witnessing any such violence, was on the lookout. "In the first few weeks in Chicago," he recalled, "every time I heard a car backfire I would jump because I thought there was some gangland warfare going on." Prohibition was still in force and the speakeasies were in vogue. "We were not regular drinkers but Neil and I decided to try one. As instructed by a friend, we went to the third floor of a large apartment block and knocked on the door. Somebody peeked out at us through a small opening in the door, then let us in. It was very posh compared to the drinking places we had known in Dundurn or Saskatoon."

Thode's financial concerns eased with some news he received after his arrival. Dr. Julius Stieglitz, the renowned head of the chemistry department, told him that he remembered his application for a scholarship, and handed him a note that directed the bursar to make the award. Harry excitedly phoned his father. "He was very surprised that they would support a foreign student right in the middle of the Depression." The bursar at this time was unusually active. Franklin Roosevelt, elected president in the fall of 1932, began his term by closing all the country's banks until they were reviewed by accountants and declared solvent. This measure put many students in a bind, alleviated only when the bursar's office took over by providing banking facilities and loans.

In a university with a commitment to exploring new directions in education, Chicago students were free to choose their research director and, to some extent, their research program. Appointed in 1929 at the age of 30, the university's new president was said to be the youngest in the history of the United States. Robert Maynard Hutchins, the former dean of Yale Law School, was causing a stir. In a memo to departmental heads, he explained that he wished to meet to discuss the running of their departments. The aging and distinguished head of the pathology department apparently did not take too well to the youthful president. He wrote back, "As for the running of the pathology department, I run it, and as for an appointment, my office hours are from nine to five."

Thode took courses in physics, applied maths, and chemistry. For an adviser and mentor in his specialty, physical chemistry, Stieglitz advised him to choose R.D. Harkins, who was a renowned nuclear chemist much sought out by students. Thode stated a preference for Simon Freed, a professor from Berkeley whom Stieglitz considered a windbag and too junior in rank. He advised Thode against the option, but Thode, fortunately, followed his initial instincts.

His research thesis proposal was to provide the first experimental confirmation of the free electron theory of metals. The theory had been developed by Enrico Fermi and Paul Dirac. They had proposed that the valence electrons of a metal behaved as a free electron gas within the volume of the metal and that they adhered to Fermi-Dirac statistics with regard to energy, momentum, and spin. The theory predicted that the positive and negative spins of electrons in clouds around the metal nuclei become free to generate strong magnetic fields as soon as the metal ions are separated beyond a certain point. Thode's work involved measuring the magnetic susceptibilities of metals at various levels of concentration.

Having observed that two professors at Brown University in Rhode Island were studying the properties of alkali metal solutions in dry liquid ammonia, Freed thought this would be a good way to achieve the different metal densities. But there were some practical problems. It was difficult to prepare completely dry ammonia, and even a trace of water would react violently with the alkali metals. Thode and Freed were eventually able to dry the ammonia by reacting it with small amounts of sodium, until there was no water left. To keep the liquid ammonia dry, a tight vacuum had to be maintained, which was also a tough challenge.

The next step was to prepare twenty solutions with different concentrations of alkali metals in ammonia, bracketing the concentration at which Fermi and Dirac had predicted major changes in magnetic susceptibility. The solutions were placed into narrow quartz or Pyrex glass tubes, sealed at the ends and divided in the middle so that pure liquid ammonia could be placed in one end of each tube, and the solutions of different concentrations at the other end.

The tubes were attached to a very delicate balance so that they hung down into the gap between the poles of a powerful electro-magnet. The magnetic susceptibilities were measured by the amounts of pull exerted by the magnet on the different concentrations of alkali-metal solution. The effects of gravity and other forces were measured by weighing each tube with the magnet turned off. The magnetic properties of the pure ammonia in the upper ends of the glass tubes were roughly equal to the magnetic properties of the ammonia in the solutions in the bottom ends, which allowed Freed and Thode to isolate the effects of the metal ions alone.

The process came with so many technical problems that it took Thode two years to get results. In the second year he was working almost around the clock. While he had enjoyed chemistry at Saskatoon, now he was captivated by it, and his fascination enabled him to put in untold hours. "I think, of all the research projects that were going on in chemistry at the University of Chicago at that time, this was the most difficult and the most challenging," Thode recalled. He was delighted that he had chosen Simon Freed over R.D. Harkins. A.C. Grubb at Saskatoon and Freed at Chicago had provided him with project work far more stimulating than he might otherwise have found. He felt that it was good fortune, he would later say, that the subjects he had chosen for his master's and doctoral work proved highly stimulating. "I was excited and dedicated to solving these problems."

In the fall of 1934, during the final stages of his work on his thesis, Sadie arrived in Chicago. She had passed a tough two years north of the border. After taking the course at the Hospital for Sick Children in Toronto, she had been unable to find a job. She had returned to Saskatchewan, where she worked in Regina at Woolworth's and at the Hudson's Bay store. She was still paying down her university debts and was intent on getting a master's degree in dietetics. As for her thoughts on Harry Thode, two years of separation had not solved much. She still was not sure about sharing her future with him, and she told him so.

When Harry heard this declaration, he told his parents, who wanted Sadie to marry Harry and had a lure to keep her in Chicago. They told her that if she enrolled in a master's program in the American city they would pay her tuition. Sadie eventually succumbed to "the pressure," as she called it, and successfully applied to the graduate school at Chicago. She boarded with another woman at first, and began attending classes and seeing Harry, though usually only in a work setting. While he was delighted she had come, his lab work was clearly his number one priority. Sadie contended as cheerfully as possible with the long hours he was putting in. He often went back to the lab late at night and stayed till two in the morning, walking home with another student, Luis Alvarez, who was to play a prominent role in the Manhattan Project, monitor the flight of the Enola Gay, and go on to win a Nobel prize in 1968. "Harry couldn't stay away from the lab," recalls Sadie. "That's why I sat on a lab stool and watched him by the hour." She thought he was working too long and too hard and urged him to slow down. Her toting of casseroles across the lawns of the university to Harry's lab got to be such a habit that the squirrels used to follow along behind her.

16

One day the lab was visited by its benefactor, George Herbert Jones, a stock-broker and leading Chicago businessman. The researchers were working on nuclear reactions in what was called a cloud chamber. Jones observed to the assembled researchers and students that the experimentation going on in the chamber was very interesting, but then asked, "What good is it?" Thode recalled how his audience of dedicated scientists were stunned that he could pose such a crass question. One had the temerity to respond, "The driving force where you work, Mr. Jones, is human greed. Here, it is human curiosity." Thode could barely keep from applauding. "As a young student, very liberal and wondering about these guys down at the stock exchange, and what they were contributing to society, I never forgot that."

By the end of the year, Harry had passed his oral examinations and successfully completed his thesis. Though never one to show much emotion, he was pleased with the accomplishment. His doctorate was conferred at a low-key ceremony on a rainy and sullen December day. Despite his new credential, Thode's job prospects were slim. Few academic institutions were hiring during the Depression. Sadie wrote dozens of letters for him to universities across the continent but received few responses. He did get one offer to teach at a Chicago high school which, given his pressing financial condition, he might have considered. But he dismissed the idea when he realized that he would have to punch a clock like a factory worker after years of a student's freedom.

While he continued his job search, Freed was gracious enough to allow him to keep working in the lab. He had his heart set on marrying Sadie and thought the time was right even if they were both unemployed. She took a little convincing. "Don't worry about the money," he told her with blithe self-confidence. "You just marry me and I'll look after the money."

To spare the Patrick family the cost of a full-scale wedding in Saskatchewan, they chose to wed in Chicago. Thode knew a classmate whose father was a minister and willing to do the ceremony. The wedding took place on February 1, 1935 at the Woodlawn Avenue Non-denominational Church. Harry's cousin Neil Jacoby and his parents, and his friend Tom Wilson and his wife, attended. No one was there from Sadie's side of the family. The couple moved into a small bachelor apartment with a pull-down bed several blocks from the university. They could not afford the rent on even these modest quarters, but Harry had succeeded in persuading the university bursar to loan them enough money to live on until he found a job.

Finally, some good news came. The Pennsylvania College for Women in Pittsburgh needed an assistant professor of chemistry. Thode was called for an interview and won the position. It was not exactly what he was looking for. The college offered no research facilities and he would have to teach subjects like geology, for which he had no training other than one university course. But the salary was a welcome $200 a month, which would allow him to start paying down some debts.

Thode accepted the offer and returned with Sadie to Saskatchewan for the summer. Thode's grandfather sold him his old car, a Whippet, for fifty dollars. A short time later it broke down near Yorkton, leaving Harry and Sadie to sleep two nights in a cornfield while waiting for a new axle to be shipped in from Winnipeg. Their belated honeymoon at Lake Madge was similarly ill-fated. Thunderstorms and heavy rains made the roads impassable and they were holed up in a small cottage. Any romantic edge the circumstances might have provided was diminished by the presence of Sadie's ten-year-old brother Terry. The boy became so frightened by the fierce thunderclaps and lightning one night that he climbed into bed with the newlyweds.

The mountainous topography of the Pittsburgh area provided the newlyweds with a change from the flat prairie to which they were both accustomed. The fashionable all women's school was located on Murray Hill, near the steel town's core. "They had excellent sports facilities where Sadie and I played tennis," Harry recalled. "We were not far from the Mellon Institute, and we could drive down Fifth Avenue to the city centre in ten minutes."

His geology course required him to take the girls on field trips. He would pack a bunch in his car, and the rest would pile into another vehicle. "I used to go along as chaperone," recalls Sadie. Harry especially enjoyed these outings. "Maybe he wished he hadn't been so insistent on marrying me," she would later joke. Thode also taught physics and chemistry, and, though there were no research facilities, he improvised his own. Neither his students nor faculty colleagues shared his passion for scientific exploration, so he just bought a tank of liquid ammonia, carted it to the campus, and continued his experiments with metallic solutions.

To earn extra money, he took on a part-time consulting job at a local rendering plant that processed beef tallow from butcher shops and sold it to soap manufacturers. They got a better price for the high-melting grades of tallow, and Thode was able to show them how to top up the low-melting fractions, which resulted in a higher average price. Sadie was an able assistant, gathering the research information Harry needed from the library. Their efforts earned a welcome $600.

During the year they spent in Pittsburgh, the city was flooded by torrential spring rains that caused the Monongahela and Allegheny Rivers to overflow. Sadie was reading in the library when the rains were so heavy the buses stopped. Advised by her parents never to take a ride from a stranger, she set out on foot to cover the long miles to the apartment. She turned down one offer for a lift home but the streets were so impassable that she finally relented and broke her vow. Much of the city was without power and traversable only by rowboat. Sadie and Harry took advantage of the opportunity to have a real honeymoon and headed to Washington for a tour of the nation's capital. It was cherry blossom season and the city wore its finest colours. In the years that followed, the couple cherished the impromptu excursion as one of the best trips they ever had.

One year at the women's college was enough for Thode. When he left Saskatchewan for Illinois, he had been inclined toward becoming a chemistry teacher, but his time at the University of Chicago had turned his tastes more toward research. His goal was to find a place to put his talents to work. The opportunity came in the summer after his first year of teaching. The annual meeting of the American Chemical Society in Pittsburgh brought together many of the leading chemists from the top universities in the country. Thode was not an aggressive young man. It was out of character for him to hit somebody up for a job, and the boldness of his next move was surprising. While at Chicago, he had come to know Weldon Brown, an earlier graduate of the University of Saskatchewan. Brown had worked with physicist Harold Urey at Columbia University while Urey was doing some of the outstanding work that would earn him a Nobel Prize, for the discovery of deuterium, the heavy isotope of hydrogen. Brown had talked often to Thode about Urey, and Thode got to thinking how wonderful it would be to work in the lab of such a dedicated and talented researcher.

Thode went to the William Penn Hotel, the site of the conference, and waited for an opportunity to approach Urey. Intercepting the eminent scientist on his way across the lobby, Thode introduced himself, and asked if there were any opportunities for work at Columbia. Urey responded with a couple of questions. "He wanted to know why I wanted to leave the college, but without waiting for me to answer he said, 'I know a number of people teaching at women's colleges and I can understand why they want to get out.' Then he asked who at the meetings knew me." Harry gave two references and Urey said he would speak to them. The next morning, Harry "met him and he said, 'Okay, you can come!' He didn't tell me what they said about me or anything. It was just like that. That's the kind of guy he was. He decided just like that!"

Thode was invited to come to Columbia as a postdoctoral fellow. Post-docs were sometimes not paid, so Thode, pressing Urey again, mentioned that he would need a stipend. Urey offered $125 a month and the deal was sealed. Urey, an Indiana native who almost flunked out of grade school, came from farming stock too. He was confident that his new recruit would know what an honest day's work was all about. From a teacher at a little-known women's college, Thode had suddenly made the jump to the research team of one of America's most renowned scientists.

Thode arrived in Manhattan the third week of September, his late appearance drawing a terse "Where have you been?" from Urey. Harry explained that he thought the university was on a quarterly semester system and that his responsibilities would begin the first week of October. "We work all year round," Urey responded, but he nonetheless handed Thode a cheque for the month of September.

Rental accommodation was ample in Manhattan and the Thodes quickly found a low-priced apartment at 123rd Street between Amsterdam and Broadway. Harry immediately plunged into an all-day work regime at Urey's lab. Thode initially worked as a research assistant, and later, when Urey became involved in isotope separation and took on a couple of other post-doc research assistants, Harry ran the whole laboratory. Left to her own devices, Sadie was initially terrified of New York but Harry's cousin Cliff stepped in to show her around, take her to the theatre, and provide tips on how safely to negotiate the huge metropolis. Having first traced out the sub-way route to Macy's department store, she ventured out on her own one day, but soon thought the better of it. "I was scared to death. I got off the subway and walked to Macy's, going through the door and right back out again. When I got back home, I cried and cried and cried. It was just sheer nerves." In time Sadie grew more confident. " I wasn't going to spend two or three years there in an apartment by myself. I finally got used to it."

Harry loved New York. "It was just fabulous. When we lived there we could go down to Times Square. We could walk all over. There was never any worry about muggings. It was cleaner. There weren't as many people around. At Radio City Music Hall, whenever there was a special show on, we could go. It was the time to live in New York."

Though he and Sadie had to live on only $125 and later $150 a month, trans-portation and food were cheap. The subway was a dime. They frequently went to Coney Island, where Harry liked to swim and have a beer, then hopped on the tram to return home. He and Sadie occasionally went out for modest dinners at a restaurant that served a good meal for one dollar. Even on his low income, Thode was able to save money. He always recalled his father's dictum: "It isn't what you make. It's what you save."

Linking up with Urey cast Thode into the field of nuclear science during a period of spectacular discoveries. In 1932, James Chadwick of Cambridge University had discovered the neutron and Carl Anderson of the California Institute of Technology had revealed the positron. The discovery of artificial radioactivity by Irène Joliot-Curie and her husband Pierre Curie with assistance from John Cockroft was another milestone. These discoveries, and Urey's work in heavy hydrogen, as Thode explained, furthered the possibilities of research into isotopes. Discovered in 1910 at McGill University by famed British scientist Ernest Rutherford, isotopes are atoms of the same element that contain equal numbers of protons but different numbers of neutrons. They have identical chemical properties but different physical properties.

Urey had demonstrated that hydrogen isotopes could be separated. At the time of Thode's arrival, Urey had already made calculations for the separation of the isotopes of carbon, oxygen, and nitrogen. The work was complicated. It required, for a start, the construction of very long columns, called fractionating columns, which he compared to alcohol stills for separating alcohol and water. Thode helped build a fractionating column that extended through three storeys. Describing the nature of the work, he recalled, "Those of us working with Urey began measuring kinetic and equilibrium isotope effects of the isotopes of carbon, nitrogen, and sulphur, then developing counter-current ion exchange systems for separating them.

"The simple separation stages had to be multiplied many times due to the decreasing magnitude of the isotope effects, as we moved to higher atomic weights. Some of these rare isotopes were present in such small traces that tons of material had to be processed to obtain significant amounts of enriched product. These difficulties were extreme for the separation of uranium isotopes, which became an urgent problem for the Manhattan Project shortly after I had left Columbia."

Working with the short-fused Urey was not always easy. Thode was thrilled when he heard that Niels Bohr, the famous Danish chemist who was the father of the theory of atomic structure, was planning to visit the lab. In the days prior to his visit, Urey noticed that Thode was having problems with the beads at the bottom of an ion exchange column. In his aggressive manner, he explained to his assistant how to fix the problem. Thode tried but was unsuccessful. The next time Urey came to the lab he was with Bohr. Noticing that Thode had not solved the problem, Urey chewed him out in the famous man's presence. An embarrassed Thode explained himself and soon won an apology from Urey.

Another well-known scientist, Rudolf Schoenheimer, came to the lab while Urey was away on a lecture tour. Schoenheimer needed some heavy nitrogen. Thode obliged, and gave him two days supply. Urey was furious when he heard from a student what Thode had done, thinking his assistant had given away all the valuable chemical.

Working in the lab required extreme diligence. Sulphuric acid was sometimes required for the release of gas up the fractionating column. Thode's job was to fetch containers of the acid from a big tank in the basement. Safety regulations required that he wear heavy cotton trousers and shirt, goggles, and long rubber gloves. Thode was properly outfitted but for some reason the sulphuric acid was exceptionally hot and, when he turned the tap on the tank, it released into the bin and exploded all over him. Thode ran to the nearby shower stall, but by then his lab coat was a mass of holes and his shoes were dissolving. The sulphuric acid had run down his gloves on to his hands and burned through his shirt at the shoulder. He dashed home to a horrified Sadie who put him in a tub, got out the baking soda, applied it to the burns, and ran to the drugstore to get bandages. She later got him to a doctor who rebandaged him and gave him a sling to wear, which Thode refused to use.

In the personal realm, Thode's time at Columbia was highlighted by the arrival of son John, at Sloan General Hospital in the Bronx on December 21, 1938. Though they did not want a big family, Sadie loved children and had time on her hands to raise them. She enjoyed wheeling the baby carriage up and down Broadway while pondering her husband's next move. His assignments from Urey were nearing completion. His two-year stay had resulted in seven papers on the basics of isotopic chemistry. He had helped design and operate systems for the separation of nitrogen-15 from nitrogen-14, carbon-13 from carbon-12, and sulphur-34 from sulphur-32. It was time to move on. Perhaps now, with the experience of working with Nobel winner Urey under his belt, Thode would be able to find a leading university prepared to hire him.

*Harry and Sadie Thode in New York City (1937)*

# Chapter Three

# Early Research and Teaching at McMaster University, 1939-1943

Thode left Columbia in December 1938 to take a job at U.S. Rubber (which later became Uniroyal) in Passaic, New Jersey, a short distance from Manhattan across the George Washington Bridge. The head of the company's lab was a graduate of the University of Chicago. Another Chicago alumnus, Thode's classmate Tom Wilson, was employed there. More coincidentally, Thode soon discovered that the fellow at the next lab bench was born and raised a few miles from Dundurn, Saskatchewan.

Thode had no long-term interest in working for U.S. Rubber; he was biding his time, making good money until he could find a decent academic post. In the meantime, he continued off-hour research in Urey's lab. Though he was no longer being paid to do the research, he was so fascinated that he was prepared to spend most of his free hours in the lab. "I did a couple of beautiful experiments at Columbia during that period," he recalled several decades later.

Outside the lab walls, the world was marching toward war, and the scientists Thode had come to know were joining the effort to produce the atomic bomb. In 1938, Otto Hahn and Fritz Strassman, researchers in Berlin who were following up on work by the Italian Enrico Fermi, discovered nuclear fission. The news was passed on to Niels Bohr in Denmark by Lise Meitner, who had worked with Hahn and Strassman before leaving Germany to avoid Nazi persecution. In January 1939, Bohr revealed the development to scientists in Princeton. Fermi was by now working at Columbia. Thode did not know him personally but heard him lecture there. Within ten days of Bohr's revelation,

Fermi, along with Leo Szilard and other Columbia scientists, was able to confirm that indeed fission was possible. It was quickly realized that if more than one neutron resulted per fission, a chain reaction would be generated, releasing energy on a colossal scale. The Columbia scientists, and others working in Paris, produced experimental evidence that secondary neutrons were emitted in fission, making a chain reaction likely.

Thode was aware of the feverish activity at Columbia but was not apprised of the details. His search for an academic post was so far disappointing, a result, according to Sadie, of his rather docile approach to job-hunting. That he was not offered a post at a prestigious university was a great surprise to many in later years. Sam Kirkwood, a leading biochemist from Minnesota who spent several years at McMaster, notes that Thode was the major dynamo in Urey's lab while some of Urey's groundbreaking work was being done. Kirkwood speculates that perhaps Thode had had a personality clash with Urey and did not get the introductions or recommendations that his mentor should have provided. Sadie discounts this hypothesis, recalling that the two scientists had always gotten along well.

In the summer of 1939, Thode received a letter from an obscure, small Baptist-founded university in Hamilton, Ontario. McMaster was looking for a chemistry instructor. Dean Charles Burke, a senior member of the science faculty, had received a strong recommendation of Thode from the University of Chicago. Thode initially rejected Burke's approach. He had only recently taken the job at U.S. Rubber and felt obliged to stick with it. But McMaster did not back down. President H. P. Whidden came to New York and asked to see Thode. They met at a hotel near Grand Central Station. Thode was sufficiently impressed by Whidden's efforts to agree to visit the McMaster campus.

Charles Burke showed him around McMaster, what little there was of it. In Hamilton Hall, where science faculty members were situated, Thode remarked on how limited the facilities were for research. He was impressed by Burke's response: "Don't you think it's high time we started something?" the dean challenged him.

Exploring further, Thode discovered a most peculiar feature of Hamilton Hall. At the time of construction the physicists wanted to have sunlight in their basement lecture room, so they had asked for a shaft that extended four floors up to the top of the building, complete with a mirror system to allow the light to travel down to optics demonstration tables in the classroom. By remarkable coincidence, this sort of structure was exactly what Thode needed for the creation of a fractionating column to be used in a range of experiments. He signed on at McMaster, partly from a lack of better offers and partly because Sadie was keen to move back to Canada.

Thode's salary as an assistant professor of chemistry was $2,400 a year, little more than half of what he was earning at U.S. Rubber. When he informed his superior there that he was leaving, he encountered perplexity at his acceptance of a post at such an unknown institution.

Looking back from the perspective of Thode's later renown, McMaster biochemist Sam Kirkwood is astonished as well. "For anyone other than Harry, it would have been committing career suicide [to join McMaster]. As well as he did in Canada, I think his contributions would have been significantly greater in the U.S. I feel quite sure that both Urey and Thode thought that he had a bright academic future on the American scene." If, as Kirkwood suspects, Thode thought he should help build science in Canada, why was he not sought after by McGill or the University of Toronto? "No one else hired by these larger, more prominent schools could have matched Thode's genius," says Kirkwood.

Few in the U.S. had heard of the Hamilton institution. McMaster had been established first in Toronto, with an endowment from William McMaster, a Baptist banker, wholesaler, Grit politician, and senator, in 1890. Toronto was the chosen setting because it was there, the founder reasoned, that Baptist and other evangelical students could best pursue a practical Christian course of education. The small university had got on its feet, attracting some respected educators, but it was greatly overshadowed by the University of Toronto. Although McMaster offered a good arts program as well as theological training, and even though a healthy percentage of the students were non-Baptist, it could not escape the tag of being a denominational school.

The First World War and recurring recessions endangered the fiscal health of McMaster in Toronto, and a raging controversy in the 1920s over the nature of its theological teachings led to pressure to relocate. Forty miles to the southwest, Hamilton was enjoying boom times, its population having doubled to 75,000 in the first decade of the new century. With pressure from Hamilton alumni of McMaster and Hamilton undergraduates who were attending the university, a citizens' committee was formed to promote the transfer of McMaster to the ambitious small city. In 1930, following a successful local fundraising drive, the move to Hamilton became a reality.

On an attractive ninety-acre site in the Westdale district of the city, five buildings were erected against the backdrop of a heavily wooded ravine. Two Gothic-style structures, one to house the arts programs and the administration and the other for science, formed the centrepiece. The other three buildings were a men's residence, a women's residence, and a refectory. On the southeast and north sides of the campus lay the beautiful 1700-acre Royal Botanical Gardens, which provided the university with one of the finest outdoor botanical laboratories on the continent.

The Depression had necessarily curtailed the university's expansion plans and brought on salary cuts for faculty. In the sciences, the emphasis was primarily on teaching, not research, but Dean Burke had built ties to the scientific and health communities. A McMaster branch of the Canadian Institute of Chemistry was founded and Burke instituted a pre-medical curriculum. The Hamilton Academy of Medicine was pushing for the creation of a medical school, but the university's pinched financial status ruled this out for the foreseeable future.

The heads of several industrial firms in the city did not think the general B.A. program included enough science courses to qualify graduates for employment. In 1939 Burke initiated a bachelor of science degree and his search for qualified teachers led him to Thode, and to physicist Gerald Wrenshall. Wrenshall soon left McMaster for the University of Toronto, but not before starting several major research projects, including one on the energy content of the atom. Knowing Thode's salary at the rubber company, Burke appreciated that he was coming to Hamilton at considerable financial sacrifice. Whidden described Thode as a "very competent looking chap and . . . very decent." Burke had many long conversations with the young Thode about his own grand designs for McMaster in the sciences and in medicine. The ambitious dean wanted to elevate McMaster far above the status of a small Baptist institution. While Thode would eventually take his own place as the major builder of modern McMaster, much of the initial vision was Charles Burke's. "You have to take him into account," observes Martin Johns, a physics professor who has watched the university grow through the decades. "He had a dream for McMaster, of which he convinced Gilmour, and Burke was the guy who hired Harry Thode. He put a lot of thought into that decision. He certainly made a right choice."

Sadie and Harry rented the first floor of a house on Beulah Avenue, below the escarpment in the reasonably well-to-do southwest area of the city. Sadie told Hamiltonians she found the small city comfortable because it was not much different from being in Saskatoon. They had barely settled in when the war broke out in Europe. Harry was twenty-nine, and eligible for enlistment, although his role as a father reduced his chances of being called up. "He wasn't the type who liked the army," says Sadie, who had two brothers in the army and one in the air force. "I couldn't get him to kill a mouse." Later on in the war, exemptions from enlistment were made for university students and faculty, especially those in physics and chemistry. These studies were considered to be in the national interest and Thode's work fitted this description.

Thode started out teaching first- and fourth-year chemistry. His office was located in Hamilton Hall, which was equipped with laboratories and lecture rooms for the study of biology, chemistry, physics, geology, and mineralogy.

The chemistry department was located on the third floor and offered a laboratory large enough for more than one hundred students. Gordon Dean, one of Thode's early students, recalls that his professor's dedication to research overshadowed his teaching interests. "As a teacher, he was always involved in some research or theory he was working on. There were times when we as students thought that his teaching was just part of the job, whereas his real love was in research." Thode's passion for research was an advantage for the students who worked with him in the lab. There, recalls Dean, Thode was inclined to roll up his sleeves and work alongside his students, while other professors remained more distant.

A custom among McMaster's student population was to leave the classroom if a teacher did not arrive within ten minutes of the scheduled beginning of class. Thode was sometimes tardy. On one occasion the ten-minute deadline passed and his class vacated the premises. At the next meeting Thode issued a strong reprimand, warning them that they were to apply no such rule to him.

Thode liked to do things his way, recalls colleague Martin Johns. "Harry was quite aggressive about his own research and that aggressiveness also translated, sometimes, into difficulties with other members of the chemistry department, at times because he did not want the rules of the department head to apply to his students. There were tension points, never very serious, but they were inevitable."

Thode had barely unpacked when he set about doing research on isotopes. Dean Burke was proud to proclaim that McMaster was the only university in the country doing such work. Thode also began teaching a night course in metallurgy for steel industry managers in the city, which brought him into contact with many men who would become important citizens and community leaders in the future.

In 1939, in search of funding, Thode visited the National Research Council in Ottawa, whose president C.J. Mackenzie had served as dean of engineering at the University of Saskatchewan. Thode won a National Research Council grant to build isotope separation columns in Hamilton Hall. In the same year he received a second grant to design and build the first mass spectrometer in Canada. Some of the leading research centres in the United States and Europe had built in-house models, and Thode had used a mass spectrometer at Columbia while working with Urey. Mass spectrometers, however, were not available on the open market. Relying on his experience at Chicago and New York and on the electronics expertise of McMaster's physics department, Thode successfully completed construction of this important instrument, which separates atoms and ions according to weight.

29

Thode was able to get some assistance from Westinghouse Ltd. in Pittsburgh. Initially he wanted the company, as is indicated in a letter to John Hipple of the Westinghouse research labs, to do much of the work. He asked Hipple to build a 180-degree mass spectrometer tube for him. When informed that Hipple did not have the time, Thode wrote back to say he would build it himself but needed some advice. How was the ground joint fastened to the lower plate? Did the Nichrome ribbed shield spread out against the outside tube? Had anyone ever used a silvered outside tube without a metal tube shield inside?

In retrospect, it was fortunate for Thode that Westinghouse could not oblige him. Building the mass spectrometer himself was an achievement to be noted. In May 1942, he announced in a letter to Hipple, "At long last we obtained enough equipment to put together our mass spectrometer." He went on to say he needed tungsten ribbon for filaments and asked Hipple to send some. Thode used the spectrometer first at the request of the University of Toronto for the analysis of sulphur isotopes. He also used it to analyze an oxygen sample in the fractionating column running through Hamilton Hall's four floors.

In addition to his National Research Council funding, Thode received financial assistance from biochemist Rudolf Schoenheimer, the scientist to whom he had earlier given some heavy nitrogen. While Thode was building his spectrometer, he saw Schoenheimer on the German's visit to the University of Toronto. Charles Best, the co-discoverer of insulin, was also present and appeared delighted to hear of Thode's project, until Thode mentioned he was doing it at McMaster. At that point, "he just lost interest completely," recalled Thode. "He couldn't understand. He thought I was going to build it at the University of Toronto. He thought I was a Toronto professor." Best excused himself, but Schoenheimer asked for more details and was prompted by Thode's reply, and his mention of being short of cash, to send along a substantial cheque. Thode never saw Schoenheimer again, although he did send his benefactor some oxygen-18 enriched water that he had asked for. The prominent German-Jewish scientist later committed suicide, in despair that his family had been seized by the Nazis.

The onset of the Second World War delayed expansion programs once again at McMaster. Thode's isotope research was to proceed on a limited basis, until history changed its course most dramatically. Following the discovery of fission in 1939, Enrico Fermi, working in Chicago, proved for the first time that a self-sustaining nuclear reaction was possible and that energy could be produced on a massive scale from atomic nuclei. The man who headed Fermi's project to build the first heavy water reactor was a Canadian. Walter Zinn, a graduate of Queen's, had worked with Fermi and Leo Szilard at Columbia before they had moved on to Chicago. Thode overlapped with Zinn for a couple of months at Columbia, but never really got to know the tall blond man who figured so importantly in the creation of the bomb.

When the Manhattan Project to produce the atomic bomb received the official go-ahead from Roosevelt's White House in 1942, it was feared that the Germans themselves were marching toward the production of a nuclear explosive. The truth was that Hitler believed that, by the time such a weapon of mass destruction could be created, the war would be over, and he never gave his scientists the resources they needed to outpace the Americans in the development of the atomic bomb.

In 1942, at the Quebec Conference, Churchill, Roosevelt, and Mackenzie King decided that a group of British and European scientists who had gathered at Cambridge would come to Canada to carry out basic research on nuclear development as an annex to, but not as a direct part of, the Manhattan Project. Canada was chosen over the United States in order to protect French patents filed in 1939 by Joliot, Von Halban and Kowalski, in the name of the French Government.

Because of his training in the analysis of isotopes with a mass spectrometer, Thode, who was only 32, was pressed by the National Research Council head C.J. Mackenzie to join what was called the Anglo-Canadian Atomic Energy Project.

In a letter written on October 9, 1942, Mackenzie worded his request vaguely. "This letter is in the nature of a preliminary inquiry in connection with a highly secret and very important war project which may be undertaken in Canada. If the present plans materialize we will need a few scientists of highly specialized training and it occurs to us that your experience and ability would make you eminently suitable for one of the posts." Mackenzie went on to say he was looking for perhaps 15 to 20 scientists who could come to work in either Ottawa or Montreal. Thode was initially noncommittal, saying he had several research projects underway, two of which were war-related. He mentioned he had his mass spectrometer operating and wanted to continue research at McMaster, but might join the project if he could continue to spend several days a month in Hamilton.

At the time, Thode was also being courted by research centres in the United States. Authorities at Oak Ridge, Tennessee, which became the largest national nuclear laboratory in the United States, offered a position that came with free housing. Columbia, which was doing key work on the project, also invited him. Thode was tempted. He had his doubts about joining the Canadian operation, which was being set up at the University of Montreal. When he went there for a scheduled appointment with Von Halban, the project head, he could not find him. Von Halban was in New York. Thode followed him there, taking the opportunity to see Harold Urey as well. Even after further meetings, he was still undecided. He tended to favour Columbia, but Sadie was adamant about not wanting to return to New York. Urey expressed the opinion that the Americans would see to it that Canada would get only the crumbs in such a grand research endeavour. In the end, Thode gave in to the pressure to remain a loyal British subject and join the Anglo-Canadian project in April of 1943.

# Chapter Four

## Secret Nuclear Fission Research, 1943-1945

Having agreed to stay in Canada, Thode made clear in a letter to C.J. Mackenzie in April of 1943 the conditions under which he would take leave from McMaster and join the Montreal team engaged in advisory work for the Manhattan Project. First, he noted, he was to receive a salary of $4,020 per annum beginning May 1. Secondly, his living expenses in Montreal would be reimbursed at the end of each month. Thirdly, he wanted permission to continue his research in Hamilton and to be reimbursed for trips back and forth to Montreal.

Thode's first assignment was to set up the mass spectrometer lab at the University of Montreal headquarters, in a brand new science building. This task would take up to a year, and Thode could see that the project's physicists, anxious to obtain uranium, thorium, and hydrogen isotope analyses, were not willing to wait that long. The solution? Since Thode had Canada's only mass spectrometer already in operation at McMaster—he had been using it to measure the relative abundances of the stable isotopes of rare gases from the Canadian Liquid Air Company in Hamilton—why not have the work done there? Administrators initially opposed Thode's idea, saying that security requirements did not allow for work outside the Montreal lab, which was under tight RCMP security. "There was a battle between the administration and the scientists," recalled Thode. "The scientists said, 'Let's get on with the job. Dr. Thode's got an instrument.'" The heated debate wore on but was finally decided in Thode's favour. Under RCMP oversight, he would be allowed to move back temporarily to McMaster, returning to Montreal on completing the necessary analyses. Thode recruited a group of seven McMaster scientists, most of them graduate students, and began work in a sealed-off section of offices on the top floor of Hamilton Hall.

By this time, the fathers of the university were coming to realize that the sciences were a new emerging academic priority. New president George Gilmour reflected that "situated as we are in an area served by heavy industry, it is almost certain that our most marked development will be in the direction of physics and chemistry . . . . I say this not because I feel that it is academically the best development, but because each university must be somewhat guided by the openings at its doors." By the end of 1943, McMaster had 250 science students, comprising 40 per cent of the student body. The development of science education sparked considerable debate. Charles Burke was concerned that the broad educational principles for which McMaster stood could be overshadowed. More extreme views also were articulated: one alumnus gave a speech calling for a re-emphasis on the humanities and the "repudiation of the false doctrine of the ultimate supremacy of the sciences."

To keep up with the science course load, the university hired Ronald P. Graham, a graduate of Queen's and Columbia, and Laurence H. Cragg, a University of Toronto graduate who was teaching at Brandon College in Manitoba. Graham soon became caught up in the war effort, setting up a special laboratory in Hamilton Hall to do research on chemical warfare. Large quantities of lethal gases were transported to McMaster. Cragg also worked on war-related assignments, including one to produce a more durable form of synthetic rubber.

Thode's research team became an annex of the Montreal laboratory, providing isotope analyses for it and, by extension, for the Manhattan Project. From late 1943 until the end of the war, Thode travelled back and forth between Montreal and Hamilton, with occasional trips to other research centres such as Columbia. Thode liked the setup. "I had my own special team and I was in a very privileged position because I didn't have to put up with the politics in Montreal and all those prima donnas. I had my own show. I got excellent financial support for the graduate students here at McMaster." He did not relish the prospect of working, however peripherally, on a bomb with untold explosive power. "I think he felt that it was his duty to do what he had to do," says Sadie. "He felt he should be doing something in war work."

Thode had a breakthrough in 1943 when the Montreal lab received uranium rods that had been irradiated with neutrons in one of Fermi's early tests in Chicago. Three young scientists in Montreal then attempted to extract fission gases from the uranium rods and to separate the krypton from the xenon, measuring their relative volumes. Thode wanted this sample, but only after they had accidentally contaminated it with natural rare gases and it was of no further use to them would they release it. In fact, they did not believe that any useful measurements could be obtained from it, as the total sample was less than a microlitre. They were wrong. From this sample Thode obtained measurements which led to perhaps the most important publication of his career. It broke new ground in both mass spectrometry and fission yield measurements. Modern users of mass spectrometers would marvel at his equipment. To obtain an isotope analysis required a manual adjustment of the electrical current that fixed the magnetic field, followed by a measurement of the ion current at that field using a ballistic galvanometer. This process would take a day to scan a mere ten mass units. The recognition of the sensitivity of the instrument, however, inspired both Harry and others to develop more user-friendly instruments that have become standard equipment in every chemistry laboratory. These have made possible tremendous advances in following progress in chemical synthesis and identification of trace compounds in living species and the environment.

The actual observations from the Montreal laboratory fission gases were the first measurements of relative fission yields that were not obtained by counting techniques. They were of unprecedented accuracy and were the first to show fine structure. The mass spectrometer became the preferred method of obtaining, first, the relative fission yields, and, later, using isotope dilution techniques, the absolute values. Much of this work was done at McMaster, and it displaced a virtual army of nuclear chemists working in this area with counting techniques as part of the Manhattan Project.

Thode's assistant on the xenon and krypton experiments was Jack Macnamara, who in the early 1950s became one of the first students at McMaster to be granted a doctoral degree. Macnamara never suspected that the work he was doing was important to the Manhattan Project. "I was never brought into any discussions about why we were really doing this other than that they were poison gases," he recalled years later. Macnamara was impressed by his mentor Thode, with whom he also did groundbreaking research on sulphur isotopes. "Harry was very patient. He let you do your own thing. He was very helpful in his own way. Various papers he had written had my name associated with his. They were really his words but he made you feel that they were yours. He wasn't a strongly demanding person at all. He was very quiet and reserved."

Macnamara could easily see that Thode was taking the lead among McMaster's science faculty. "He was the prominent one among all of the chemistry and physics professors, organic or inorganic. The others didn't really have the command to get you excited about what might come out of the work that you were doing. He seemed to have a feel about what we were going to find before we found it. I think you have to give Thode the full credit for the change of the university from a theological college to a science college." (McMaster University, of course, despite Macnamara's terms and the large change in the 1950s, historically never has been simply either "a theological college" or "a science college.")

Gordon Dean, one of the group doing the war research, saw Thode as "a very hard worker and a genuine person; he expected you to be the same." Thode was diligent and professional, recalls Dean, and discussions with him were usually strictly business. For lunch, the group met at a separate table in the corner of the refectory. "We didn't debate the issue of the atomic bomb," says Dean. "We weren't delighted in any way that this could be used to kill people. I think we all regretted that it was used." Thode seldom talked about the war or progress on the Manhattan Project. The secrecy was such that none among the McMaster group had any idea what was going on in Los Alamos, or how much they were contributing to the development of atomic weapons. "We knew we were associated with the building of the A-bomb, but whether we were actually contributing much was difficult to say," recalls Dean.

Thode was disappointed by the lack of co-operation between the Montreal project and the corresponding laboratories in the United States. He wrote to Mackenzie at the National Research Council, expressing his regret and saying "we must get on the best we can." Thode hoped that his solid relationship with Urey's laboratory at Columbia, which he had supplied with heavy water oxygen, would return the favour by providing information Thode needed on the Nier deuterium mass spectrometer. If Thode did not get this cooperation, he would have to drop other important work and design a deuterium mass spectrometer of his own, he warned. In a letter addressed "My dear Thode," Mackenzie replied that it was unlikely that the Americans would oblige. Despite Thode's frustration with the Americans and the overall heavy security, his lab did further work on xenon isotopes and their report was sent to the Manhattan Project headquarters at Los Alamos.

Thode's rising stature was recognized when he was nominated as a fellow of the Royal Society of Canada in 1943. His contribution to the Manhattan Project was small when compared with that of Walter Zinn, but years later he was told by his American colleagues that they had been surprised by the amount of detailed information that the McMaster group had obtained from the small samples that they had been allowed to work with. "Thode's role was important," notes Mel Preston, a nuclear physicist who joined him at McMaster in the 1950s, "in that they were able to detect which isotopes were more significant in the fission process."

The work consumed Thode. In keeping with the university's Baptist origins, McMaster's faculty members and students were expected to attend a daily chapel service at 11 a.m., where the professors took turns reading the prayer and announcing the hymn. Thode often skipped this service and ignored the prohibition about working on Sundays. Though intensely focused on his research projects, Thode was not the most organized man and was easily frustrated by bureaucratic regulation. "In the lab, Harry had students who were doing both classified and unclassified work and he had an awful time trying to operate, as everybody had access to everything," recalls Martin Johns. "I don't think he ever really approved of all these stupid regulations. His secretary sat in a window overlooking the sundial of Hamilton Hall and she could see the [RCMP] police cars [when they came to] check up [on security] and I can remember her saying, 'Everybody to their stations, the police are coming.' And they never got caught. They were always in the right places."

Thode did most of his travelling between Montreal and Hamilton by train. One night no sleeper car was available, so he took a more expensive roomette. When he filed his expense account, the Montreal authorities reprimanded him for profligacy. An irate Thode wondered how they expected him to sleep in a regular passenger seat all night and still be fresh for work in the morning. He could hardly believe they were so upset over the cost of a train berth, engaged as they were in multimillion-dollar research project.

The Quebec Agreement between Churchill and Roosevelt provided for limited contact between those working in Montreal and those in the U.S. In 1943, Thode needed to consult with the University of Chicago's Arthur Dempster, who was an expert in the field of mass spectrometry. Just to speak to him, Thode had to go all the way to the top, to General Leslie R. Groves, who was commander of the Manhattan Project. A letter came, allowing Thode limited clearance. When he arrived in Chicago, he was escorted by an army captain to the Manhattan Project's local headquarters. The army captain initially monitored the discussions between Thode and Dempster but, becoming bored with all the technical talk, he went off to lunch with a warning that they should keep their conversations within the guidelines they had been given. Thode and Dempster quickly joined another table of scientists, including Leo Szilard.

Back at the office, Dempster handed Thode the files he needed and left the Canadian alone. At the soft drink machine, he bumped into Robert Moon, an old Chicago colleague who had helped build a cyclotron at the university. Moon wondered what Thode was doing in the restricted area. When Thode told him of General Groves's letter, Moon mistakenly assumed he had a general clearance and invited Thode into his office for a chat about nuclear technology. On the way out of the restricted area, security men asked Thode whom he had visited. Moon was later called to explain this lapse in security. For a time it appeared that Moon's security clearance might be in jeopardy, but the matter was eventually cleared up. Thode was to confide to one of his colleagues that his best conversations at the project's Chicago labs took place in the washroom, "because they wouldn't follow us in there."

Security precautions extended even to the RCMP's interviewing Thode's neighbours, as they reported to Sadie after the war. She did not inquire as to the details of her husband's work, because "he felt I was safer if I knew nothing. So I literally did not know what he was doing. He didn't know himself why he was doing certain things. In a way he was doing his research blind." Thode experienced stress at work, but preferred to keep his anxieties hidden as much as possible. "If he started to laugh, he suppressed it. If he started to smile, he suppressed it," recalls his wife. While he loved research, Sadie is still uncertain whether his work on the Manhattan Project actually appealed to him. "I felt that if he had his choice he would have preferred some other type of work," she says.

Students and faculty at McMaster suspected that highly secretive work was being done at Hamilton Hall. Rumours circulated that heavy water was being prepared for the new nuclear plant at Chalk River. At times bells would ring and research assistants would become agitated. One day in early August 1945, Martin Johns was invited by Thode to accompany him on a visit to a farm he owned on the shores of Lake Erie. They turned on the radio in Thode's car and heard the shocking news that the atomic bomb had been dropped by the Americans on Hiroshima. Johns could not detect Thode's reaction. Because the American team had kept the Canadians so much in the dark, Thode had not had any prior knowledge of the atomic attack.

C.D. Howe, minister of reconstruction in the King government, made public the McMaster research and other work by Canadians on the atomic bomb shortly after the Americans' use of the weapons. The bombs, which turned Hiroshima and Nagasaki into rubble and incinerated tens of thousands of innocent civilians, triggered the surrender of Japan and the war's end. Their use necessarily engendered controversy. Towards the end of the war, Thode was convinced that Germany and Japan's defeat was inevitable. Critics of the bomb's use argued that American president Harry Truman could have chosen to drop the bomb on a more desolate Japanese island, as a warning to the enemy of the phenomenal new power the Americans possessed. They asked why it was necessary, after detonating the bomb on Hiroshima, to drop another one three days later on Nagasaki, without waiting for the Japanese response to the first attack.

Thode's colleague Dick Tomlinson recalls discussing the bombings many times with Thode. Thode concluded that a demonstration bomb probably would not have worked, says Tomlinson. Thode believed that the Japanese were simply too determined ever to surrender and that, because the Allies had only two atomic bombs, they did not have the luxury of using one for show. Perhaps Truman should have waited longer before dropping the second bomb, but without these weapons, Thode believed, the war would have dragged on. The result might have been an even greater loss of life, although it would have been mainly among the military rather than among the Japanese civilians vaporized in Hiroshima and Nagasaki.

Thode tended to confine his thoughts on the atomic bomb to the practical rather than the ethical. After the war he summarized his views in six concise points:

"Atomic bombs can now be made cheaply and in large numbers."

"They will become more destructive."

"There is no military defence against atomic bombs and none is expected. Other nations can rediscover our secret processes by themselves."

"Preparedness against atomic war is futile and, if attempted, will ruin the structure of our social order."

"If war breaks out, atomic bombs will be used, and they will surely destroy our civilization."

"There is no solution to this problem except international control of atomic energy and ultimately the elimination of war."

The lasting controversy over the dropping of the bomb on Japan arguably does nothing to detract from the importance of Thode's work for the development of nuclear science. Martin Johns speculates that Thode's contribution to mass spectroscopy was so impressive during this period that it should have been considered for a Nobel Prize.

Johns's admiration for Thode as a scientist does not extend to his abilities as an administrator. In 1945, Thode had invited Johns to work in his lab. Johns wrote back to him accepting, but did not get a response. Johns spoke to someone else in the department, who checked with Thode, who confirmed that he wanted Johns to come. Johns worked in the lab for weeks without a word being said about his salary. Finally, one day, Thode asked him if he was getting paid. Johns said he had not received any information on the subject. Thode then offered him about three times what Johns had expected. Johns naturally was delighted at the extent to which Thode went to bat for his people. "I got a grant to build a beta ray spectrometer. It was only half what I needed. When I asked Harry what to do, he said, 'Spend it as fast as you can and ask for more.'" But, even with the help of more grants, Johns found that he needed $10,000 more. "I went to Harry with this problem and he said, 'Forget it, I'll put $10,000 in your account.' This is one of the great things about Harry. He was unselfish in dealing with new people. I don't know of anyone else as generous as he was."

39

Reconstruction minister C.D. Howe heaped praise on Canadian efforts in nuclear science, and the press reception was equally glowing. Shortly after the close of the war, the *Hamilton Spectator* headlined a story "McMaster Scientists Give Help in Splitting of Atom: Hamilton's University Aids in Great Discovery." The lead paragraph read, hyperbolically, "McMaster University scientists working in the deepest secrecy . . . have aided in what is now being hailed as the greatest scientific discovery of all time."

An article in the *Toronto Star* on August 13, 1945 began by saying: "While the mighty little midget, the atomic bomb, is being dropped on Japan and shattering open a new era for this universe, the Canadian scientists who played a leading role in its development are taking a well-earned rest. . . . They had literally gone into hiding nearly three years ago—and stayed there until the powers that be told them their job was completed—for now." Thode was quoted as saying, "It was high pressure, every minute. They need a rest now —and they're taking it." He said that he would not be able to rest until all his colleagues had been advised of what he termed "the success of the bomb."

Whatever Thode's feelings about Truman's decision to deploy the bomb, he was relieved by the war's outcome and heaped praise on his research team. His work had put McMaster on the map as a university strong in scientific research. Initially, he had been expected to move the research centre back to Montreal once its assignment had been completed, but his team's outstanding success made it possible to urge that the centre should remain at McMaster until the close of the war. The stage was now set for several decades of leading nuclear research at McMaster. Moreover, Harry Thode, in just six years at the university, had proven himself an invaluable faculty member, one to whom the senior administrators were already looking for future leadership.

*Sir John Cockcroft, Director of the Manhattan Project (seated, right, with Dr. Thode), visits in August of 1945 to learn about wartime research being carried out at McMaster. Standing (from left to right): R.C. Hawkings, D. Roberts, H. Duckworth, R.L. Graham, and G. Dean.*

*M.W. Johns*

*Harry Thode (1945)*

# Chapter Five

## International Science, Espionage, Thode's Research in the Early Postwar Years

Many scientists resent a climate of secrecy and restriction being created around their work, believing themselves to be at a remove from politics. They prefer to work in an atmosphere of fraternity and co-operation, bolstered by the notion that borders should not get in the way of scientific progress.

Bruno Pontecorvo had been one of Enrico Fermi's students in Rome. The two men left Italy in the late 1930s, Fermi going to Columbia and on to the University of Chicago, and Pontecorvo to Texas. There the tennis champion from Pisa worked in the oil exploration business, inducing radioactivity in the walls of drill holes to determine mineral content. After the war broke out, he was recruited by the Anglo-Canadian Atomic Energy Project and worked in Montreal and Chalk River, where he helped design the first nuclear reactors. American authorities looking for nuclear scientists had taken a pass on Pontecorvo. He was not an American citizen and security clearances were strict. The American attitude, recalled Thode, was that they would be happier if Canada took him.

Thode found the debonair Pontecorvo to be very much in the thick of things. He was among those trying to determine how much uranium was necessary to get the critical mass needed to produce a chain reaction. When Pontecorvo moved on to Chalk River, Thode came to know him better, and the two men would go swimming together: "I would be lying on the beach with him and we would be discussing science," Thode remembered. On these occasions Pontecorvo "never discussed politics," recalled Thode. Laura Fermi, married to Enrico Fermi, confirmed this impression in her book *Atoms in the Family*. After the war, Thode continued to correspond with Pontecorvo and assisted him on some matters. In letters, he addressed his friend as "Dear Ponte." In one, Pontecorvo asked Thode for specimens of the non-metallic element boron. Thode, who was analyzing samples of boron with his mass spectrometer, promised to comply with Pontecorvo's request.

In 1946, Thode invited the Italian to give a lecture at McMaster. Afterwards Thode inquired as to Pontecorvo's plans for the evening. The enigmatic scientist replied he must first check on his wife (she was Swedish) and his children. To Thode's astonishment, he had left them for hours in a parked car at a service station, on a cold November day. Thode acknowledged about scientists that their dedication to their work often caused them to neglect their families, but even he found Pontecorvo's action extraordinary.

Pontecorvo left Canada for England two or three years after the war to work as a professor of physics in Bristol. Not long into the job, he visited his family in Italy and his wife's family in Sweden, then disappeared without a trace. For two years no one knew his whereabouts. The next time Thode heard of him was in 1950, when Pontecorvo's picture appeared with an accompanying story in a Moscow newspaper. He had been in Russia for two years, helping the Russians develop their own A-bomb. Washington labelled Pontecorvo the world's "second deadliest spy." The first ranking was given to Klaus Fuchs, the German-born British citizen who had worked on the Manhattan Project in Los Alamos, and who was later convicted of treason for providing atomic secrets to Moscow from 1943 on.

Pontecorvo had been raised in poverty, and Thode speculated that his Communist leanings grew out of his early experiences. "There were people at Chalk River who thought that maybe his wife was a Communist ideologue. There is a possibility that she was able to persuade him that this was the future." Thode believed that Pontecorvo came to regret his decision to defect to the Soviet Union. "Obviously the Russians were offering something . . . a home, big salary, everything," he noted.

In a 1955 letter printed in *Pravda* and *Izvestia*, Pontecorvo, who had been awarded the Stalin Prize, issued a bitter attack on Western atomic weapons development. He explained that he had fled the West because he believed that the United States was preparing to use the bomb again. The military use of such weapons made him "ashamed of my profession." He explained that he became a member of the Institute of Physical Problems of the Soviet Academy, which promoted the use of atomic energy for peaceful purposes. He called on scientists around the world to work for a ban on atomic weapons.

Remarkably, Thode met up with Pontecorvo again. In 1959, accompanied by E.W.R. Steacie, who was now head of the National Research Council, and some other scientists, Thode was invited to Moscow by the Soviet Academy of Sciences to work out an exchange program with the West. At the Soviet nuclear facilities at Dubna, northeast of Moscow, Thode later recalled how, when he was walking around the grounds looking at the buildings from the outside, he "spotted Pontecorvo across the street. He was hesitant at first, but broke out into a big smile when Steacie held out his hand. He was happy to see us and full of enthusiasm as usual, telling us about his scientific projects." Pontecorvo lunched with the Western scientists but declined a dinner invitation, saying he was making arrangements with his family for an extended trip. Thode later concluded that he was probably travelling to China with a delegation of Soviet scientists to help the Chinese produce their first atomic bomb. Thode was told that Pontecorvo's wife was in a mental hospital. Years later, Pontecorvo was awarded the Lenin Prize. He later died of leukemia.

Pontecorvo was not the only nuclear scientist sympathetic to the U.S.S.R. with whom Harry Thode was personally acquainted. Alan Nunn May lived in the same building in Montreal as Thode did during his brief stay there and taught the Canadian how to make tea in the proper British way. May was working as a professor of physics at Cambridge University when several prominent European scientists moved there to escape Nazi persecution. When these scientists left for North America during the Battle of Britain to work on the Anglo-Canadian project, the British government sent along someone it could trust to accompany them. May was the chosen one. Thode found him to be "a very normal human being whom you could get to like," and, like Pontecorvo, "he never discussed politics."

Later, Thode found out why. May, a balding moustachioed man with wire-rimmed glasses, knew Jules Gueron, the French radiochemist in the Anglo-Canadian group, from their days together at Cambridge. One day May inquired as to what his friend was doing. "I'm separating uranium 233," Gueron replied, then explained the procedures on a blackboard, pointing out the beaker that contained a substantial amount of valuable uranium. "The next day Gueron came into the lab and could not find his uranium. The facility that had the uranium in it was there, but there wasn't any uranium," recalled Thode. Mortified by the loss, Gueron offered his resignation.

In September 1945, Soviet defector Igor Gouzenko revealed to Canadian authorities that security at the Montreal and Chalk River laboratories had been breached from within. A few months later, May, now back home in Britain, was identified as a traitor. He pleaded guilty to violating the Official Secrets Act and was sentenced to ten years in prison. It was disclosed that he had forwarded the stolen uranium to Fred Rose, a Communist member of the Canadian parliament, who then turned it over to the Soviet embassy. May, who had passed other secrets to the Soviets, had done so, he explained, because he "felt that this was a contribution" he "could make to ensure the safety of mankind," referring to a belief held by many in the postwar years that world security was endangered if it were only the United States which possessed the atomic bomb.

Following his release, May became head of the physics department at the University of Ghana, where by coincidence Thode later was to attend a conference. May was reluctant to face his old colleague, although Thode was less censorious of May's actions than May might have imagined. "None of us approved of these defectors," said Thode. "To us it was just being dishonest when they had pledged themselves to secrecy . . . and also disloyal to their country. Having said that, all scientists believe in the international aspect of science; it's the exchange of information that leads to progress and [ideally] there shouldn't be any secrecy. . . . We were possibly less shocked by these defectors than the public at large."

The Gouzenko-Rose scandal put a cloud of suspicion over the Montreal lab and anyone who had had anything to do with it. Thode was among those called to testify before a government commission investigating the espionage activities. The situation was a difficult one for Thode. Reputations could be seriously tarnished merely by association. Thode had to rely on the hope that his involvement with those under suspicion of espionage would be properly understood as being strictly professional and that he had had no reason to question the loyalty of his erstwhile colleagues. While Thode did not say much to Sadie, she knew that the inquiry "was very serious business. He was at the end of his tether. He was getting so many calls, from Ottawa, Chicago, New York."

Thode even became concerned for his physical safety at McMaster, his wife recalls. He knew the RCMP had him under surveillance and, in a way, he was relieved because this offered him some protection. The Mounties talked to Thode often, and he was called twice to Ottawa. On one occasion, he was asked to go to Toronto for a formal interrogation. Laurence Cragg of the McMaster chemistry department was also called in. Cragg was not part of Thode's nuclear research lab, but he had done some war research into poison gases. Thode insisted to the Mounties that Cragg act as a witness during his own interrogation. The two men were more bemused than concerned, Cragg later recalled. The questioning was very general. "I think they found it nonproductive," Cragg says. "We weren't rated very high as suspicious characters. . . . Harry and I were amused because we knew we were absolutely blameless in this regard. Their suspicions, if they had any, were allayed."

At their home in Westdale, the Thodes entertained several Russian scientists. The Soviet women were impressed by the plethora of goods in the home, particularly the electrical appliances. One perplexed wife told Sadie, "You have a washing machine and dryer, a dishwasher, and two cars—yet you have no servants!"

Although Thode normally shied away from political debate, occasional musings suggest that he leaned toward internationalism, perhaps even embracing the idea of an international governing body. In a postwar speech he was quoted as advocating "a limited form of world government—with the door open for Russia to come in—even if it is five or ten years before she does that." A proposal for the international control of atomic energy had been placed before the Atomic Energy Commission of the United Nations in June 1946. The Russians had insisted on the destruction of all atomic bombs before any control agreement was put in place. Thode labelled this insistence a manoeuvre to delay an agreement. When the Russians exploded their first atomic bomb three years later, his suspicions were confirmed. Thode's prediction that atomic bombs would be used as a matter of course in future wars has fortunately proven incorrect, as Thode himself was to see during the Korean war.

Thode's outlook on atomic development was not all gloom and doom. In another address, he forecast some of the benefits that could come from nuclear power. "When man first discovered fire, he probably got his fingers burnt, and no doubt was frightened. He soon learned however that a controlled fire could keep him warm. Later, molecular fire, the burning of coal, led to steam engines, steam plants, and railway locomotives. Today, we are in the bonfire stage with atomic fire. Pound for pound, an atomic fire is one million times as effective as a molecular fire. Primitive man with his bonfire was not able to foresee present-day uses of molecular fire; neither are we able today to predict the uses of atomic fire. That atomic power plants are possible seems a certainty, although there are many costly experiments necessary before a commercial plant can be engineered."

In nuclear medicine, Thode knew that radioactive isotopes would be used to diagnose and treat cancer and other diseases. In 1944, he and Ron Graham obtained evidence of the existence of a new radioisotope, Krypton 85. In later years, Thode would find great satisfaction in seeing Krypton 85 used in medical research and in industry.

While Thode continued to study nuclear fission for some twenty-five years following the war, the emphasis in his research by the late 1940s had returned to his first love, stable isotopes in nature. In 1949 he built the first of a series of mass spectrometers capable of measuring isotope ratios with a very high level of precision. With these he turned his attention to variations in the abundance of the sulphur isotopes, sulphur-32 and sulphur-34, in a wide variety of naturally occurring materials. Thode found that, almost everywhere he looked, sulfides were depleted in the heavier isotope, while the sulfates were enriched. He quickly realized that this was a consequence of a difference in the rates of reaction of the two isotopes in the low temperature bacterial reduction of sulfate to sulfide. This immensely important work was published in three landmark papers: "Natural variations in the isotope content of sulfur and their significance" in 1949, "The distribution of sulphur-34 in nature and the sulphur cycle" in 1950, and, in 1951, a paper presented to the American Chemical Society which set out the complete biogeochemical cycle of sulphur and the historical record of the isotope ratios of sulfate and sulfide backward in time. With this work, Thode clearly established himself as the father of sulphur isotope geochemistry, a field which has had immense practical significance and has been extended by others beyond his own research contributions.

Thode's last paper, "A stable isotope study of pyrite formation in the late pleistocene and halocene sediments of the Black Sea," was published in 1996, a year before his death and almost fifty years after the pioneering paper of 1949. In the intervening years, he pursued many applications of sulphur isotope geochemistry, including ore formation, fossil fuel deposits, pollutant sulphur in sediments, the isotopic composition of sea water and, following man's landing on the moon, the isotope abundances in lunar rocks. In addition, his laboratory was the first to demonstrate terrestrial variation in the isotopic composition of boron and selenium.

Thode's record of accomplishment would be considered outstanding for any person devoted full-time to research. But, for much of his career, research was something that he carried out in such spare time as he could find apart from his heavy administrative responsibilities. He, of course, was fortunate in having excellent research associates, and he had the gift of being able to select capable colleagues to whom he delegated some of the non-research responsibilities. Nevertheless, the scope, quantity, and importance of his scientific contributions are remarkable.

Thode's stature at McMaster grew because of his war research work, but his goal of making the university an institution for first-class scientific research faced many obstacles. Traditionalists such as H.F. Dawes, the head of the physics department, frowned upon the idea of too much emphasis on graduate studies.

The university's original goal—to provide for an educated Baptist clergy and to be a "practical Christian school of learning"—over a half century had led to a major emphasis on undergraduate arts and science education, plus theological education for a relatively few students. This goal was strongly adhered to by the traditionalists. One vociferous opponent of Thode's ambition to create a first-rate science school charged the administration with wilfully violating the institution's historic Baptist principles. Highly advanced scientific research should be the province of other institutions, Evan Gray argued, in an ill-disguised repudiation of Thode's war-related research. Historian Chester New weighed in against the university's broadening into the Ph.D. programs that Thode was advocating. Famed political economist and communications expert, and a graduate of McMaster, Harold Innis took the occasion of receiving an honorary degree at McMaster to warn against the university's becoming too beholden to the visions of businessmen and industrialists, the very people Thode was cultivating to play an increasing role in McMaster's development.

The conflict over the direction of the university came to a head in June 1945, with a vote on reorganization proposals that would allow McMaster to receive government financial support. President Gilmour urged that the proposal be accepted, recognizing that the university could not move forward in the postwar world under the old model of church and private funding. A counter-motion, led by Evan Gray, was defeated, much to Thode's relief. His ambitions for McMaster could now be given free rein.

# Chapter Six

# The 1947 Founding
# of Hamilton College,
# The Start of Doctoral Work

With the arrival of large numbers of war veterans, the McMaster student body expanded by more than 50 per cent, from 546 in 1940 to 853 in 1945. New revenues allowed for physical expansion of the small university, which had seen the addition of the Drill Hall during the war years to accommodate the training of undergraduate soldiers and airmen. Plans were set in motion for a divinity college and for a new library to replace the cramped quarters in Convocation Hall. For the admirers of McMaster's hitherto uniform architectural aesthetic, there was disappointment that the grand and noble Gothic structures of University Hall and Hamilton Hall would not be copied in the new buildings. Dreams of a university that looked like Princeton were surrendered to economic realities and the eventual result was the architectural diversity, integrated by intelligent landscaping, that is evident in the visible campus today.

The growth in student numbers occasioned the need for new faculty members. Thode, technically on loan from the university to the nuclear project until 1947, sought to improve the quality of the physics and chemistry departments. One scientist he had in mind was Robert Moon, the nuclear physicist who was a fellow graduate student during Thode's doctoral study at Chicago. Moon had since constructed at Chicago a cyclotron, which is an accelerator in which particles move in a spiral path under the influence of an alternating voltage and a magnetic field. Moon's cyclotron was the second to be built in the United States.

Thode saw Moon as a potential future chairman of McMaster's physics department. Though faculty recruitment was chiefly the job of the dean of arts and sciences, Charles Burke happily ceded the responsibility in science to Thode. Burke had not had time to keep up with advances in scientific research and was less qualified to assess the best candidates. With Moon's apparent acceptance of the Thode offer, H.F. Dawes, the department head, felt his toes being trampled on and did not hesitate to make his views known. In a letter to Chancellor Gilmour, his sarcasm dripped from the page: "After almost a forty-year sojourn in the wilderness I hope he [Moon] will be the Joshua to lead the department of physics into the land of promise." Dawes's sense of insult led him to see Gilmour's action as "a distinct blow" to him, and a clear indication that the president was "not quite satisfied with" what he and others had been able to do and could do in the future. In a later missive to Gilmour, Dawes speculated on whether it was wise to put all of McMaster's scientific eggs in the nuclear basket. He acknowledged Thode's successes in the field, but felt that specialization might diminish the growth of other discipline like meteorology, electronics, and solid state physics.

While he received little in the way of comfort from Gilmour, Dawes perhaps found some degree of satisfaction in the eventual result of Thode's dealings with Robert Moon. Having indicated his willingness to accept Thode's offer, Moon now hesitated. One of his expressed concerns was a postwar ruling of the American Energy Commission forbidding any American scientist from teaching abroad on any subject that might relate to the design or construction of a nuclear device. This edict had particular resonance with Moon, in light of the grilling he took after his Manhattan Project meeting with Thode.

Thode immediately went to bat for his friend, petitioning all the way to the Minister for External Affairs, Lester Pearson, to have the ruling challenged. Thode was vigorously opposed to the Washington edict because of the limitations it set on scientific interchanges. At the time he stated publicly, "If Moon as a scholar can't come to Canada, our science will be sterile." Pearson cooperated, taking the complaint all the way to American Secretary of State Dean Acheson, who assured him that Moon would not be prosecuted if he took the job at McMaster.

Still, Moon dilly-dallied. At one McMaster meeting he appeared half asleep. Many observers had the impression that he was waiting for a better offer from an American university. George Gilmour, who had a good sense of humour under his puritanical exterior, grew impatient with the changeable Moon, once asking colleagues, "What phase is the Moon in now?" The local press got involved, further highlighting the controversy, and Thode himself was beginning to doubt Moon's suitability, calling him a good physicist but "a little immature in other respects."

The news of Moon's pending arrival had encouraged people like Martin Johns, a top young researcher working at Chalk River, to join the physics department. In the end, Moon stayed in the United States, and Thode endured long-standing embarrassment over the matter.

If George Gilmour was put out by the Moon affair, he could add the episode to a short list of minor grievances he held against Harry Thode. At the end of the 1944-1945 academic year, Harry and Sadie hosted a party for graduate students and their wives and girlfriends. It was at the Thode home, where McMaster's strict non-drinking rules on campus did not apply. The party was a tame affair and well conducted, but liquor was served. The word got back to Gilmour that the Thodes had hosted a wild party, and he made his displeasure known. On the next social occasion when they met him, the Thodes tried to moderate his annoyance with friendly overtures, but Gilmour snubbed them. The cold shoulder treatment continued for many weeks, and the Thodes, who found Gilmour to be brilliant but stiff and unapproachable, decided to let the rift heal with time.

These were modest setbacks, and Thode had too many credits in his ledger to diminish his rising stature. He was now well-placed to spearhead a drive to broaden the mission of McMaster to include Ph.D programs and the creation of a separate science college at the university. But if the sciences were to grow, they needed more funding than was then available to McMaster as a denominational institution. Without the large government subsidies available to other universities, McMaster had to look to private sources, mainly Hamilton's captains of industry. Thode, who by now had moved from the rank of assistant professor to full professor, had been cultivating his relationship with these men for some time. Often he and Sadie were guests at dinners hosted by important industrialists like Frank Sherman of Dofasco, or William Pigott, who owned one of the city's dominant construction businesses. "Harry got to know the industrialists very well," recalls Sadie. "The night course he taught in metallurgy turned out to be a good opening for him." Sadie does not think that her husband was ever much of a social climber, but he was a hard-headed realist who knew that cultivating such a network was an important part of his job. She did not suspect during those postwar years that Thode had any ambition to become president of the university. If he did, he never confided it to her. His eventual ascent came about as a result of a logical progression of events, she says, and those who knew the methodical and generally modest Thode tend to agree.

Thode gradually was able to sell the idea for a separate science college to the administration, with the support of Dean Charles Burke and the local industrial establishment. At a meeting at the private Tamahac Club, a board was nominated to oversee the creation of the new affiliated college, whose goal was to train men and women in the basic sciences to a level of excellence unsurpassed in the country. In affiliation with the rest of the university and remaining under the authority of its senate in matters of academic standards and degrees, Hamilton College was authorized to manage its existing science programs and to devise new ones. To do so it was directed to solicit external funding from government and private sources. George Gilmour remained the chief administrator of the university; Charles Burke was the first principal of Hamilton College; and Harry Thode was his vice-principal. Burke had clearly been won over to the paramountcy of the role of research at McMaster. The university, he stated, "is not merely a teaching organization . . . passing along to students information. . . . gleaned by others. But she is also attacking . . . the secrets of nature and adding year to year a great deal of information to the sum total of the knowledge of mankind."

In 1947, Hamilton College was still only a paper institution, but, by 1948, the nucleus of the board of governors had been nominated and an application had been made for a charter. When Charles Burke fell ill, Thode took the leading role in the college's development. A capital founding fund of $2.5 million was set as the goal and solicitations were successfully underway by 1948. The promotional booklet for the campaign clearly stated that the science college had no religious affiliations. In the view of many at McMaster, Baptists had given way to industrialists and bureaucrats. Gilmour was quoted as saying that "industries, business houses, and government agencies today are willing to undertake a generous share of the total responsibility which private benefactors and old endowments can no longer carry alone."

While planning for Hamilton College, Thode faced smaller problems, in his chemistry department. In a report submitted to the chancellor in May 1949, he complained that his department was woefully understaffed. Faculty were faced with added teaching loads, new administrative duties, and added responsibilities in professional societies, while at the same time trying to do their research. "The point is, of course, that members of the staff cannot continue this pace for long. Already certain important work has had to be sacrificed, and the chemistry plans for Hamilton College have not progressed as rapidly as they should," Thode warned. His report listed all the activities of the teachers of the department and included a list of the research papers he had published himself over the previous year. There were seven: "Mass Spectrometry and Nuclear Chemistry," "Mass Spectrometer Determination of the Half-Life of Xenon 133," "Variations in the Abundances of Isotopes in Nature," "Mass Spectrometry," "Natural Variations in the Isotopic Content of Sulphur and their Significance," "The Isotopic Effect in the Decomposition of Oxalic Acid", and "Natural Variations in the Isotopic Content of Boron and its Chemical Atomic Weight." The dictum "publish or perish" was never intimidating to a scholar with Harry Thode's capacity for intellectual rigour, long hours, and hard work.

In issuing his appeal for more faculty members, a need he described as "critical," Thode compared McMaster's physics department with that of the University of British Columbia. At the graduate level, he noted, McMaster had half as many students but less than one-third the staff. The undergraduate comparison showed a similar ratio. Although genuinely concerned about the teaching loads of his staff, Thode himself did not like to teach. He once confessed to a colleague that he felt that his classroom skills sometimes lacked the flair needed to get his message to a roomful of undergraduates. His awareness of his own pedagogical shortcomings was one reason that he preferred research.

Charles Burke passed away in 1949, and Thode took his place as principal of Hamilton College. While moving ahead with plans for the college's development, he pressed for the creation of a Ph.D. program in chemistry. There were then only a few universities in Canada (Toronto, McGill, University of Montreal, Laval) offering doctoral programs, and McMaster's administrators did not contemplate such a move for a decade to come. But Thode was intent on boosting the college's image quickly. "It is my feeling," he wrote to an old friend, "that, with a few Ph.D. students around, the morale of the whole place will be raised and new and better courses will develop naturally."

In his history of McMaster entitled *McMaster University: The Early Years in Hamilton 1930-1957*, Charles Johnston wrote that "for some time [Thode] had been reacting against an academic colonialism at McMaster that decreed that advanced graduate studies be left to other institutions, notably the University of Toronto." Thode was further pushed to move ahead on doctoral programs by the news that the University of Western Ontario was starting one in chemistry. Thode was aghast that an institution that he judged so ill-qualified was undertaking such a program. To back his claim for the doctoral program, Thode reached out for letters of support from prominent scientists like Harold Urey and E.W.R. Steacie of the National Research Council. Steacie was entirely supportive, writing to Gilmour that Thode and his department had established an outstanding reputation for research in their specialized field: "It would be of great value to the country as a whole to have students trained to a further extent under the direction of Dr. Thode and the others." E.W. R. Steacie said it was unfortunate that just as McMaster students got to the stage of real accomplishment they often moved to other universities for their doctoral work. In another letter, Steacie told Thode that he was "horrified" that Western had undertaken such a development. "I don't know of any place less competent to do it."

Arthur Bourns, recruited from McGill to the chemistry department in 1947, got behind Thode's drive for the advanced programs. "He believed very strongly that we should have a strong research presence, not just for chemistry or physics, but for the whole university," Bourns recalls. "Coupled with that was the development of graduate studies because graduate studies and research were almost one and the same thing." In his struggle to develop doctoral programs in the sciences, Thode was up against many faculty members in arts, as well as science, who feared that the university's emphasis on excellence in teaching would suffer if research and advanced studies came to predominate.

Once the idea was accepted in principle, debate followed over the requirements for a Ph.D. in chemistry at McMaster. Harold Urey told Thode not to worry about required courses so much. "I learned one valuable lesson at California," Urey told him, "and that was that it was not necessary to sit in formal lectures in order to acquire knowledge." He advised that Thode show the courage to demand fewer formal requirements for the Ph.D. than was the norm at the big U.S. schools and to accept only a small number of candidates, so that staff could devote a large amount of time to each student. Thode was also in contact with Princeton to find out how the prestigious institution ran its doctoral program in chemistry. Professor Hugh Taylor of the Ivy League school sent Thode a detailed outline complete with a strong endorsement for McMaster's moving ahead with the plan. Taylor said that those who were against the proposal should face up to the fact that any university that did not move ahead with such graduate instruction in those areas where it was highly competent would then lose its esteemed faculty members to other institutions. Arthur Bourns recalls using the Princeton calendar as the basis for the program that he and Thode drafted and ultimately had approved by the university senate. In 1950, McMaster accepted its first doctoral students, Gordon Lindsay and Jack Macnamara, both of whom became important research chemists.

With this move, the institutional character of McMaster changed almost overnight. Soon there was an all-out battle over doctoral programs for other departments. It did not take long for sparks to fly over a perceived conflict between the university's mandate as an undergraduate teaching institution and what it was now attempting to become, a preeminent advanced research establishment.

Thode, who was as much a physicist as a chemist, thought it absolutely essential for the Ph.D. program in chemistry to be coupled with one in physics, and he now undertook another campaign. "Harry could see the importance of a cluster of programs that reinforced each other," says Bourns, "something that is now generally accepted." Thode got the doctorate in physics approved in December of 1951; botany and zoology programs soon followed. Decades later, Bourns recalled the proud day in 1951 when Gordon Lindsay and Jack MacNamara graduated as McMaster's first Ph.D.s in chemistry. Lindsay stayed on at McMaster an extra year doing research, because at the time at which he had met all of the academic qualifications the senate had yet to approve the doctorates.

Lindsay revered Thode, or "the boss," as he and other students called their research director. His enthusiasm was inspiring and contagious for these students. "He'd come up to you and his eyes would be sparkling and he would just be so enthusiastic about some research topic that somebody had published. He could see where we could do better or contribute something in that field. He'd get almost nose to nose with you and he'd just get so excited."

Thode showed no evidence of ego to Lindsay or the others and never discussed his wartime work with them. Nevertheless, Lindsay recalls an atmosphere of pride on campus that McMaster had contributed so significantly to the wartime effort and that it was continuing to conduct innovative research. "You have to remember isotopes were a completely new field," Lindsay says. "Mass spectrometry was just coming in. We had skilled people in the machine shops that built the parts." Thode and his people also were the leaders in the field of dating stones and rocks by their isotopic ratios. If Lindsay has one criticism of his former mentor, it is that Thode stayed so focussed throughout the rest of his research career on this one area, at the expense of others where his talent might also have flourished.

With Thode's encouragement, Arthur Bourns developed a research program in which the stable isotopes of carbon, nitrogen, and sulphur were used in the study of organic reaction mechanisms. This field of study drew on Thode's interest in the effect of isotopic mass on reaction rates, and on the unique mass spectrometer facilities that Thode had built at the university.

Thode spotted unusual talent in Bourns and did his best to further it. In 1955, Bourns spent a year at University College of the University of London in Cambridge on a Nuffield scholarship. Upon his return Thode revealed his plan to create a faculty of graduate studies at McMaster. He asked Bourns, whom he had made chairman of the graduate studies committee in 1950, to help him establish it. Gilmour had already approved this Thode initiative. He deferred frequently to Thode, who was fortunate, notes Bourns, in having such a supportive president: "Gilmour was not a visionary but he was a man of deep insights. [He had] a willingness to recognize qualities of people and the vision of others and he supported Harry. If Harry had served under a president with lesser qualities than Gilmour . . . then he might not have been able to realize [his vision]. Gilmour's support in those early years was very crucial."

*The Chemistry Department, McMaster University: (from left to right) Laurie Cragg, Dean Charles Burke, Arthur Bourns, Harry Thode, Ron Graham (1948)*

*Harry Thode raised purebred Herefords at his Selkirk, Ontario farm*

# Chapter Seven

# Developments in Science and Engineering in the 1950s

As principal of the newly established secular Hamilton College, Thode had a mandate to expand the science programs of McMaster. Hamilton Hall was originally planned to serve the general science needs of 150 students, but in the early postwar years it was clear that enrolments would soon far surpass this number and new facilities would have to be constructed. Thode's first infrastructure priority was for a new home in which nuclear research in medicine, physics, chemistry, and geology could be carried out. Planning began with his sending some sketches of the proposed new structure to the National Research Council, which was to undertake some of the funding. His plans were gently criticized by National Research Council head C.J. Mackenzie, who told him, "You are paying a great deal for architectural features which are not necessary in a laboratory building." Canadian universities, he said, could no longer afford the elaborate Victorian Gothic or Romanesque architecture favoured by earlier generations.

McMaster's Nuclear Research Building was completed in 1951 at a cost of $650,000. Designed with major input from Thode himself, it accommodated advanced atomic research facilities for a few dozen graduate students and faculty. Among its features was the first radioisotope laboratory of its kind in a Canadian university. The building included a "hot lab" with walls one foot thick and lined with lead. A vault with six-inch walls housed radioactive raw materials from Chalk River. The structure's rooms were designed so that, in the event of a nuclear accident, only the room in which the explosion took place would be contaminated. At its opening Thode said the building symbolized "Canada's coming of age" and a new era of science in the country.

"The last 25 years belong to the United States," Thode told a luncheon gathering. "Who knows but that the next 25 will belong to Canada, or at least Canada will share them with the United States?"

The Nuclear Research Building made possible a major expansion in Thode's pioneering work in mass spectrometry. Thode received strong assistance from Harry Duckworth, the physics professor in Hamilton College who had worked with Thode in the mid-1940s, before moving on to Wesleyan University in Connecticut. During Duckworth's absence, Thode determined that new strength was needed for the physics department. During a discussion with Martin Johns, he mentioned that Duckworth had the skills the department needed as it looked toward the future. Johns agreed, even though he knew Duckworth would outrank him in the departmental hierarchy, whereupon Thode picked up the phone and called Duckworth at Wesleyan. When Duckworth returned to McMaster, he brought with him a highly sophisticated mass spectograph that he had designed at Wesleyan. He became chairman, and it was his leadership, with the full support of Thode and Martin Johns, that developed the physics department into one of the few best in the country.

In mass spectrometry, greater accuracy of measurement requires larger instruments. Thode, Duckworth, and their colleagues set to work on constructing a mass spectrometer that filled a room twenty feet wide. In this machine, electrically charged atoms, each weighing a few millionths of a millionth of a millionth of an ounce, were accelerated by 100,000 volts to a speed of about three million miles per hour. They were then shot at this speed into the magnetic field of a large electro-magnet. The magnetic field pulled sideways on the atoms so that they travelled in semicircles, the light ones being pulled onto a smaller curve than the heavy ones.

Throughout the early 1950s, Thode provided important information for the Defence Research Board in Ottawa on the Soviet Union's bomb development program. With McMaster doctoral student Carmen McMullen, Thode examined atmospheric particles for uranium and plutonium content. To obtain samples, the RCAF aeroplanes flew over the Northwest Territories, close to the Soviet Union. Filters on the wings of the aircraft collected the material for radiochemical work at Chalk River and mass spectrometry at McMaster. These activities were all top secret, and the results were relayed from the Defence Research Board to the Pentagon.

Thode and McMullen thought their data provided evidence that the Soviets had tested a thermonuclear bomb. "We had a pretty good idea from the numbers we were getting as to what was going on because we were analyzing for the ratio of plutonium," recalls McMullen, "and if you found an enhancement of the successive isotope, well, you knew something significant was being done . . . . We didn't do calculations on what the megaton strength of the bomb was or that sort of thing."

Thode and McMullen would not learn for decades that their research had indeed confirmed the timing of the USSR's first hydrogen bomb. Nikita Khrushchev announced in 1955 that the Soviets had detonated a hydrogen bomb. In his memoirs, published in the 1990s, Soviet physicist Andrei Sakharov revealed that the exact date of the first explosion was August 12, 1953. When he was apprised of the information in the book, Thode rushed to see McMullen. They looked up the dates of their research in their files. To their delight, they matched Sakharov's timing. The American and Canadian militaries' obsession with secrecy meant that Thode and his colleague were kept in the dark about the value of their researches for almost 40 years.

Thode's constant involvement in nuclear science required that he monitor his exposure to radiation. Observing the work of the medical doctors he visited, Thode became alarmed at the lack of protection patients received when undergoing x-rays. He worried that physicians did not understand the dispersion capacity of radiation. At the time, shoe stores used x-ray equipment to take exact measurements of children's feet, but Thode wisely refused to allow his children to be put through this procedure.

Nuclear medicine began to intrigue Thode, who knew that radioactive isotopes were being used for medical purposes at the University of Chicago. An outstanding Hamilton internist, Charles Jaimet, had attended a biochemistry conference at Harvard University and grown excited about the possible uses of radioisotopes as a diagnostic tool in medical therapy, particularly with regard to thyroid diseases. Thode was introduced to Jaimet by his own physicians, and he accompanied the internist on a visit to the Chicago medical school, where Jaimet talked to people involved in this type of work.

Thode became keen to establish a radioactive isotope laboratory for clinical use at McMaster. The scheme's opponents focused on McMaster's lack of a medical school, making it, in their view, an unsuitable home for such a clinic, but Jaimet was able to convince them that the school's prominent role in wartime nuclear research meant that it had a significant number of prominent nuclear physicists and chemists. Thode then had to overcome the opposition of the Department of Health and Welfare in Ottawa, which he did by persuading the bureaucrats that, in Canada, it was only McMaster that had the facilities and faculty members to do what was being done at Chicago, Harvard, and Brookhaven. In the end, Charles Jaimet became the first medical director of the groundbreaking new clinic, which was set up in a temporary army barracks.

"You may be wondering," Thode told the Hamilton Academy of Medicine, "why I, as a physicist and chemist, should be speaking on the clinical uses of radioisotopes. At the moment, I am wondering myself. However, I have been interested in the production properties and uses of radioisotopes for almost 15 years and I suppose it is only natural that I should be interested in the clinical uses of isotopes as well." He further explained that McMaster had a responsibility to the community to see to it that the medical profession had the tools and personnel to make use of breakthroughs in his science labs. In the back of his mind, he was contemplating the future establishment of a medical school, but he knew that the time was not yet ripe.

Sam Kirkwood was one of the science faculty members who took part in the operation of the clinic. He did some innovative work in radioisotopes, but credited Thode as the pioneer in their practical application. "Not only was Harry ahead of the Canadians, he was neck and neck with the U.S. [scientif-ic] avant-garde. The whole raison d'être of the Mayo Clinic was the diagnosis and treatment of thyroid disorders. This is what made it famous in the beginning. Harry was right up there with the Mayo boys!"

Director Charles Jaimet came to earn the respect of the pure scientists. "Not only was he of high intellect," recalls Kirkwood, "he had avoided the usual medical indoctrination concerning superiority. He knew what he knew and knew what he did not and was a very willing learner." Thode had ready access to radioisotopes produced at Chalk River, and the group built and maintained their own instrumentation. "I think there is little question that we had the most efficient operation on the continent," recalls Kirkwood, "which meant in the world at that time."

Thode went about the business of introducing bold change in a quiet, undemonstrative manner. His commitment and understated enthusiasm were contagious, notes Arthur Bourns, who eventually became McMaster's first chairman (and then dean) of graduate studies. "You got caught up in his vision and wanted to share in it. When he talked about his research or about establishing an engineering school or Ph.D. studies, he was a salesman. Oh, absolutely." And Thode's salesmanship extended beyond his academic confrères. "He got out into the community and got to know the C.E.O.s of the major companies and he sold them on what McMaster could become and on the importance of research to the institution . . . . He was a very complex person, quiet and modest. You would be impressed [at first] by his warmth, but once he got going you would be impressed by his vision."

It was Thode's ability to "instill confidence" that earned him support from Hamilton's leading corporations, including Stelco and Dofasco. Bourns recalls that the industrialists believed that "here was a man who, given the resources, would succeed. They were confident he would, whereas the rest of us might have had the same vision but not the personal qualities that would excite others and make them share that vision."

A relative newcomer to the faculty when Thode appointed him head of graduate studies, Bourns developed a close rapport with his mentor, sharing both some overlapping research interests and a modest taste for liquor. "In the Baptist institution liquor was taboo and I didn't have a car," recalls Bourns. "Finally I discovered a man who wasn't a teetotaller and who had a car." Chancellor George Gilmour never took a drink, so it was left to Thode to preside over any occasion where liquor was served.

Looking ahead, Thode could see the need to acquire extra lands for campus expansion, and he had his eye on a large tract to the south, bordering on Main Street. He approached Gilmour about securing it for the university but Gilmour stalled and the Ontario Government eventually built the Hamilton Teachers' College on the choice acreage. In due course, in the late 1980s, after the college had been closed and St. Mary's Secondary School had outgrown the premises, Alvin Lee, as president, persuaded the Government of Ontario to turn the property over to McMaster. It is now the site of several important developments.

Thode, with the help of Duckworth and others, kept up his drive to attract first-class scientists to McMaster. Mel Preston was an assistant professor of physics at the University of Toronto in the early 1950s. When he began receiving inquiries from McMaster, he wondered, "Why would anyone in his right mind leave U of T to come to this dump?" With the enticement of "building the best physics department in Canada," Thode convinced him to come. Preston took him at his word, and proof of the university's serious intention emerged soon after he arrived. He informed Thode that at Toronto he had had access to a computer, the first university computer in the Commonwealth, and that he needed one for his work at McMaster. Thode soon fulfilled his wish.

Though reserved and diffident on the surface, Thode was strongly competitive, says Preston. He wanted to be first in his research, to beat others to the punch. But his drive to excel did not extend to his withholding information from other scientists who might be doing similar work, as was done frequently by some of his peers. Thode was no Machiavelli, Preston notes. Rather he was a top-notch researcher motivated by intense curiosity. For men like Thode, "one of the most interesting and satisfying things," says Preston, "was to learn something new about the world. Your science is one of the things that makes life worth living."

During the 1950s, Thode was running Hamilton College, doing his own research, constantly in demand to give speeches, and orchestrating the construction of a $1.3-million physical sciences building. He was a fellow of the Royal Society of Canada, and a member of the National Research Council, the Defence Research Board, and the Hamilton Mountain Sanatorium Board. "He seemed to have endless strength and he slept like a log," Sadie remembers. "He had a way of separating his worries into different compartments." Sadie admits to sometimes resenting that Thode's staggering workload left him little time for home life. When they were newlyweds, he had taught Sadie how to play chess. Family games became a Sunday afternoon tradition that the couple shared with their sons. But eventually Thode's professional commitments took their place. "I really resented it when he started going to meetings on Sunday," Sadie admits. Harry did attend the United Church every Sunday morning and took his children "through the Sunday school routine," but "he was never really into it," says son Pat. "I think he was trying to do the right thing with my mother by going to church."

Paradoxically for such a busy and productive man, Thode was a skilled procrastinator. Letters and invitations went unanswered for weeks. Good researchers are not necessarily good administrators, and Thode was not a man with a tidy desk or sharp memory for office detail. His secretaries, despairing of trying to get answers from him to the constant requests he received, often appealed to Sadie to get him to make a commitment. Thode hated writing letters, preferring to deal with people directly. He was much more persuasive in person than on paper. This quality, his gentle force of persuasion, was key to his success. "If there was one thing I got from my father," recalls Pat, "it was how to deal with people. He somehow got others to work for him, and with him, and they enjoyed doing that, even though he put enormous pressure on them."

Thode's communication skills did not extend to giving speeches. He could never master the knack of using a text while at the same time communicating personally with the audience. He would write out his speeches at home, take them to the podium, and then speak off the cuff.

Thode's limitations as an administrator or maker of speeches were not paralleled in his stature as a researcher. In 1954, he was accorded one of the highest honours in the field of science when he was named a fellow of Britain's Royal Society. The Society, founded in 1662 for the purpose of improving natural knowledge, included 500 members worldwide. He was the first member of McMaster ever to be so honoured. President Gilmour made note of the occasion by saying, "I am even prouder, if that were possible, of my distinguished colleague than I have been during all the years since he joined McMaster University staff in 1939 as a young and relatively unknown physical chemist."

The postwar arms race and the launch of Sputnik by the Russians in 1957 increased the need for scientific exploration, which confirmed the validity of Thode's vision for McMaster. But George Gilmour worried that the balance was now tilting too far toward science and creating a stagnation in the arts and humanities. "If only Arts and Divinity could be put in as good shape as Science," he wrote to financier and university benefactor Cyrus Eaton, "I would feel much happier at this desk."

Thode displayed no animosity toward development in the arts disciplines and their important role, but he was convinced that the sciences offered McMaster great opportunities to excel and expand. Other Canadian universities had preeminence in the arts and humanities; McMaster's main chance to make a mark in national and international academia, he felt, lay in the sciences. Following the construction of the new Physical Sciences Building, which also housed a planetarium and a science library, the board of governors, at Thode's prompting, authorized the establishment of an engineering school with four-year programs leading to a bachelor's degree. Chemical engineering and electrical engineering were given priority, in keeping with McMaster's strong pure science programs in chemistry and physics. Thode appointed John W. Hodgins director of engineering studies and later made him dean of the faculty. "The major objective was clear," said Thode. "The engineering school must be first-class and modern in every respect, ready to face the changes which occur in this rapidly changing world. It was clear to us that such a school should provide engineering courses well integrated with science and, most important, should have a well-balanced teaching and research program."

In addition to chemical and electrical engineering, the new faculty was to have degree programs in metallurgy, engineering physics, and mechanical engineering. Civil engineering was a later addition. The initial plan was to admit 500 engineering students. Thode wanted a different kind of engineering school, one that was more scientifically oriented than the one at the University of Toronto, which emphasized technology. While Hodgins erred in the odd appointment, Thode's vision was largely achieved, and engineering became one of the leading fields of study and research at the university.

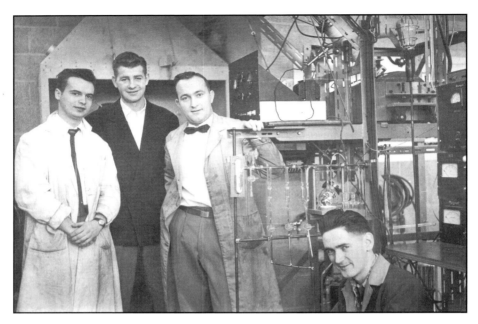

*Dr. Thode's lab in the early 1950s. Shown here with the Von Ubisch Spectrometer (from left to right) are A. Dean (technician), T.J. Kennett (student, now Professor Emeritus, Department of Physics, McMaster), C.C. McMullen (research associate, now Professor Emeritus, Department of Physics, McMaster), and D. Harvey (student)*

*Preparing for a day of combining at Selkirk, Ontario farm (1956)*

# Chapter Eight

## Nuclear Science and the McMaster Reactor

Complementing Thode's drive and competitiveness were a keen eye for talent and an equally discerning capacity for spotting prima donnas and laggards. His correspondence reveals an evaluation of a Dr. Starke, a chemist with a controversial reputation who spent a year at McMaster before running afoul of Thode. Starke was peripherally tied to the Atomic Energy Project. The National Research Council wanted Thode's opinion of him. Thode did not want Starke to stay at McMaster or, for that matter, in Canada. Knowing that Starke had his eye on a chair at a university in Germany, Thode advised C.J. Mackenzie to let him go. Starke, he observed, suffered from a persecution complex. Thode had offered him complete academic freedom, but he was unable to attract students and refused to burden himself with any university responsibilities. Starke was a better than average chemist, Thode acknowledged, "but certainly not so good that we should put up with all his eccentricities. . . . Starke was prejudiced against the Americans when he came to Canada and his opinion of them has certainly not improved. He has a tendency to emphasize certain undesirable features of American politics, etc., and to discount  all their good points, thus convincing himself that they are almost as bad as the Nazis."

Thode was not unaware of his own deficiencies as an administrator, and was smart enough to seek out people to back him up. In the first class he taught at the university in 1939, Thode had taken note of a fourth-year student named Mike Hedden, who was holding down a full-time job at Stelco in addition to his studies. Hedden would work the graveyard shift, "and yet have enough energy and get enough sleep during the extra eight hours that he could spend six or eight hours at McMaster University getting his fourth-year program. . . . I marvelled at him."

Later Hedden became an employee of Central Scientific, a subsidiary of a science products company in Pittsburgh, and on his sales rounds would visit McMaster. With the creation of Hamilton College, an opening existed for an administrative officer and Thode chose Hedden. It was one of the wisest decisions he ever made. Hedden was warm, diplomatic, remarkably efficient, and schooled in the sciences. He would stay up all night if required to get the work done. Recalls Richard Tomlinson. "All Thode had to do was say, 'Look, Mike, we ought to do this' and it was done."

Thode looked for quality people, regardless of their political or national affiliation. He brought postdoctoral fellows to McMaster from around the world. During the McCarthy period in the mid 1950s in the U.S., when witchhunts of those suspected of being Communists or Communist sympathizers ruined many promising academic careers, Thode was appalled by the excess of paranoia that led to the persecution of colleagues like Martin Kamen, the brilliant biochemist who in 1940 made the important discovery of carbon-14, an isotope of carbon later used to date archeological artefacts. At the opposite end of the spectrum from Thode's own political non-engagement, Kamen had been a supporter of the Spanish Loyalists during the Spanish Civil War and he expressed sympathy for the Soviets after their tremendous losses fighting on the Allied side against the Germans during the Second World War.

In 1943, while working at a radiation lab at the Berkeley campus of the University of Southern California, Kamen attended a reception for his close friend, violinist Isaac Stern. Dr. John Lawrence, who had discovered the benefits of radioactive phosphorous for the treatment of leukemia, was also present. During the evening, the Russian vice-consul in San Francisco asked Kamen if he could help in obtaining radioactive phosphorous for the treatment of a Russian official suffering from leukemia. Kamen obliged and the Russian vice-consul later invited him to dinner at a well-known San Francisco restaurant. There the two men were under surveillance by American security agents who were compiling a large file on Kamen, believing that his casual links with the Russians constituted a grave security risk. On a later occasion Kamen and Thode bumped into each other at a scientific conference in Atlantic City. During a stroll along the boardwalk, Thode noticed that two men appeared to be tracking them. When they entered a coffee shop the two sleuths followed, seating themselves at a nearby table.

Kamen was eventually dismissed from his position at Berkeley on the grounds that he was a security risk. After a period of anxiety and despair, he was able to obtain a position at the medical school of Washington University, but the harassment continued. Called upon to testify before the House Un-American Activities Committee investigating alleged Communist infiltration into the American government, Kamen became the subject of a so-called exposé in the *Chicago Tribune* that labelled him a "Russian spy."

Thode knew the charges were a travesty and that Kamen was a man of higher quality than any of his accusers. Thode believed that Kamen had missed winning a Nobel Prize because he had allowed the name of his associate, who got the prize, to appear ahead of his own on a research paper. Kamen believed this self-effacing gesture would help his colleague gain a tenured appointment. Kamen eventually won a lawsuit against the Chicago newspaper and was able to restore his damaged reputation.

During the early 1950s Thode and his colleagues began to contemplate the installation of a nuclear reactor on the campus. The Nuclear Research Building was a first step in providing the facilities to carry on a nuclear program. The logical second step was "a research reactor on campus, where we could produce our own radioisotopes and provide beams of neutrons on a grand scale for producing nuclear reactions." Furthermore, reasoned Thode, "McMaster was ideally suited in regard to industry. Although it was too early to predict what industrial uses would pay off, it was a certainty there would be industrial uses of neutrons and gamma rays on a large scale."

Canada's only nuclear reactor was at Chalk River and university researchers had some access to it: "However," noted Thode, "Chalk River cannot be expected to exploit their nuclear reactors in all fields of research nor can they provide the training in nuclear science and engineering which is required." Moreover, he argued, Canada had a large uranium mining industry and was quickly becoming the largest producer of uranium in the world. "It therefore seemed to us high time that at least one university in Canada had a nuclear reactor facility."

No other university in the British Commonwealth had its own reactor. "It was, at the start, truly an outrageous idea," recalls Harry Duckworth, "to build this dangerous nuclear reactor on a university campus surrounded by residential housing." But Thode, added Duckworth, was determined to put McMaster on the map and a reactor was guaranteed to accomplish this goal. Once people got over the notion that the reactor was a wild idea, recalls Duckworth, they could see the advantages that would flow from it. What really made Thode spring to action, according to Richard Tomlinson, was the rumour that McGill had similar plans. Thode was not about to be beaten by McGill. In nuclear research, McMaster was to be preeminent. His attitude, recalls Tomlinson, was that "if anyone is going to have one, it has to be us." The ready access to the strong neutron beam flux that an on-campus reactor would provide would have enormous applications in all fields of science, engineering, and medicine.

In Thode's words, "the reactor was intended to expand the program of fundamental research in nuclear science; expand the facilities for training personnel in all fields of science; make possible applied research employing the techniques of nuclear science of interest to industry; and benefit the university's medical research program."

The campaign to install a nuclear reactor at McMaster dramatically underscored the university's evolution, in less than two decades, from a modest church-run institution to one of the nation's leading scientific centres. The reactor would provide, as the *Hamilton Spectator* put it, "a huge new field for the man behind this transition to exercise the 'plain human curiosity' that led him from a Saskatchewan farm to the title of 'Mr. Isotope of Canada.'"

Thode had little difficulty in convincing President Gilmour and other prominent members of the board of governors of the wisdom of the venture. Frank Sherman, who headed Dofasco, and Hugh Hilton, president of Stelco, also came quickly on side. Thode had Duckworth run a series of lectures for engineers and other interested parties to help gain community support. Duckworth explained the industrial advantages that would flow from having a reactor. Thode and a delegation of supporters went to Columbus, Ohio, to view a working reactor in a private laboratory that was part of a research institute. "We walked around there and collectively sized it up and thought, well, if they could do it here we could do it at McMaster," recalls Duckworth. Thode also went to Kiev, capital of Ukraine, to visit its university reactor, where he was shocked by the lax safety and security procedures, concerns that he vowed to make a priority at McMaster.

The estimated cost to install the reactor was $2 million. On the assumption that both industry and government would benefit, $1 million was to come from private sources, $1 million from government agencies. The most significant private donor was Eldorado Mining and Smelting Company, which pledged $500,000, but reneged without explanation the day before McMaster's board of governors was scheduled to give final approval to the project. "I guess they just changed their mind," was all Thode could speculate. He worried that Eldorado's decision might lead to an unravelling of the entire project if other donors became jumpy. Thode telephoned his longtime friend and colleague, E.W.R. Steacie, president of the National Research Council, and explained the dilemma. The N.R.C. was one of the backers of the project and Steacie, Thode knew, was enthusiastic about it.

Under the administration of the National Research Council was the Banting Foundation, which was mandated to provide support for important Canadian science research projects. But no grant had yet been drawn from this fund because of the tight conditions imposed. In effect, it was a lending agency and few, if any, researchers were in a position to repay the funds provided. Steacie's solution was simple. He negotiated a proposal to lift the repayment condition and rushed an Order-in-Council through Parliament to ratify the change. The foundation could now deliver the money for the reactor. Within a week, Thode had the pledge for his missing half-million.

The appointment of architects to design the reactor facility was virtually pre-ordained. W.R. Souter and Associates enjoyed the sustaining advantage of having previously designed the Nuclear Research Building. The reactor, in a sense, was an extension of that initiative. As well, Thode had long been educating Souter about nuclear reactor construction, taking him to Cornell University to explore hot lab facilities for handling isotopes and to Chalk River to view its operations.

The chosen model for the McMaster reactor was a pool-type reactor of the type already operating in Columbus, Ohio. It was the most flexible of proven designs for research and teaching. Another similar model was in operation in Geneva, Switzerland. In a pool-type reactor the fuel elements are assembled at the bottom of a deep pool of water. This water, in addition to cooling the fuel and slowing down the neutrons, further serves as a shield to protect operating personnel from radiation.

Thode's administrative right hand, Mike Hedden, had the requisite scientific background skilfully to negotiate the specifications for the nuclear hardware with the supplier, American Machine and Foundry, whose head of marketing was young Vincent Massey, a nephew of the then current Governor General of Canada. Hedden and Thode established warm relations with Massey, who was a forthright and tough negotiator.

For the actual construction of the reactor building, Thode and his colleagues wanted a Canadian company and selected a local firm, Pigott Construction. Concern was expressed whether Pigott had sufficient expertise with the special reinforced concrete required for the reactor's security. Few North American contractors had experience with using the required barium instead of calcium carbonate cement. Company head Pigott was offended by the insinuation he might not be able to handle the job and a quarrel ensued. Ultimately, as Thode and others had feared, the company did have problems with the barium cement. Meanwhile, as work was being completed on the reactor, McMaster faculty members from many scientific disciplines— botanists, zoologists, biochemists, chemists, physicists, metallurgists, and geologists—were laying out plans for its use.

With its location in a densely populated area of 300,000 people within a ten-mile radius, the reactor naturally provoked public concerns over safety. The devastation wrought by nuclear energy on Hiroshima and Nagasaki only twelve years earlier was not forgotten. But most citizens were persuaded—this being long before the days of Three Mile Island and Chernobyl—that the safety risks were minimal and that the reactor would bring great benefits to the community. "The reactor," Thode explained to audiences of concerned Hamiltonians, "is designed in such a way that even in the unlikely event of a sudden rise in the rate of energy released, and the controls failed to operate, the chain reaction would be brought to a stop, since the surrounding water would reach boiling point and the steam would displace the water. Once the water is removed from around the fuel elements, the neutrons are no longer able to produce fusion in further atoms, and the process stops."

Thode was highly confident on this score, because, before going ahead with the reactor, he had awaited the results of a lengthy experiment in Idaho, where scientists had tested a pool-type reactor for all possible malfunctions. In the Borax experiment, as it was called, one hundred failed attempts had been made to prompt an excursion or blow-up. He pointed out that McMaster had been involved for more than 15 years in basic nuclear research, and that now the benefits from exploring more deeply into the nature of matter—and from tapping the energy to be derived—would provide a new source of electric power and a new means of diagnosing and treating many diseases.

Thode added that, on the economic side, Canada now had a billion-dollar uranium mining industry and would soon be the largest producer of uranium in the world. "The stakes are very high, and Canada cannot afford to be merely a bystander in this new development. It is clear, therefore, that we must remain in the forefront of medical research and, most important, we must train research workers capable of utilizing and developing the potentialities of nuclear energy. It is, therefore, high time that Canadian universities had modern equipment in the field."

Thode had organized the first postwar international conference on nuclear chemistry. He had participated as a Canadian delegate in the second United Nations conference on the peaceful uses of atomic energy. As a great supporter of the international free flow of scientific information, he was delighted at the sight of scientists from 66 nations meeting in Geneva to thwart secrecy on the nuclear issue. He had disapproved of the major powers, the United States, the Soviet Union, and Great Britain, keeping hidden their studies on the release of useful power from controlled fusion reactions.

The potential horrors of nuclear energy had not dimmed Thode's enthusiasm for further nuclear research and development. "Atomic weapons have completely changed military strategy," Thode told an audience in St. Catharines, "and, we hope, have become war deterrents. In my opinion peaceful developments of atomic energy will have an even greater impact on our everyday lives."

The three R's of atomic energy — reactors, radioisotopes, and radiation – would lead, he continued, to substantial benefits. He went on to outline a rosy future for nuclear power stations. Through the example of his own laboratory at McMaster, he could tell his audience in great detail the benefits of nuclear energy as applied to medicine. The application of radioactive iodine as a treatment had largely come to replace standard thyroid operations in the U.S., Canada, and Great Britain. Radioisotopes were also being used to detect heart defects and to develop improved techniques in the production of foodstuffs and other agricultural products. They were being put to several important industrial uses such as tracing oil through pipelines.

After some delays, construction of the reactor, which began in August 1957, was completed at the end of 1958. The reactor came officially into operation in April 1959. With Prime Minister John Diefenbaker in attendance at its inaugural ceremony, Thode explained that the reactor had "gone critical." "This means that a controlled self-sustaining nuclear chain reaction is now maintained in the reactor core and as the uranium 235 fuel is burned up in a kind of neutron fire, energy is released and neutrons produced on a large scale. This means we now have available on this campus a large source of neutrons and radiation sources for teaching and research."

Thode's speech was typically matter-of-fact and, with regard to his own overwhelming contribution to the reactor's installation, disarmingly modest. The indisputable fact is that without Harry Thode, no reactor would have been built at this time. The installation of the reactor was "a phenomenal accomplishment on the part of Thode, absolutely phenomenal," recalls Arthur Bourns. "To sell the industrial community on the need for this university to do it first, the first in a Commonwealth university, at a cost that was far beyond anything any university in the country had put in place. It was a remarkable vision."

In 1959, Thode journeyed to the Soviet Union with a delegation led by the National Research Council president E.W.R. Steacie to explore a possible exchange of scientists between the Soviets and Canada. Under Soviet president Nikita Khrushchev and U.S. president Dwight Eisenhower, relations between the superpowers appeared to be warming, a trend that Thode certainly welcomed. During the visit to Russia he grew to appreciate the prodigious talent of Soviet scientists and was stimulated by his discussions with Russian academicians, while sensing some of their frustration with the Communist system under whose constraints they operated.

Thode was especially fascinated by physicist Peter Kapitza. A future Nobel Prize winner, Kapitza was born in Russia, and did postgraduate work in Britain. At Cambridge University, he became renowned for his studies in low-temperature physics. In the mid-1930s, perhaps unaware of the extent of repression in his homeland, Kapitza made the mistake of returning to Russia to visit his relatives. The visit proceeded, but while Kapitza was waiting at a railway station, his train for Warsaw about to pull out, he was approached by two men and informed "Mr. Stalin wants to see you." Kapitza never saw the West again.

Kapitza told Thode that many diplomatic channels had been unsuccessfully engaged to secure his release. Even Churchill made an appeal. But Kapitza's scientific talents were deemed indispensable to the U.S.S.R. Kapitza was amply rewarded for his value to the state. He became head of a lavishly equipped physics institute. He was given a home and a chauffeur. He received several salaries: for his position at the institute; as vice-president of the Soviet Academy of Science; as editor of a scientific journal; as a lecturer at the University of Moscow. Thode asked him, "Who gets paid more in the Soviet Union than senior scientists like you?" Kapitza replied, with a twinkle in his eye, "Ballerinas!" Thode was impressed at the priority given to science in the Soviet Union as compared with his own country. Kapitza explained that whereas in the West scientific development was random and spontaneous, in the U.S.S.R. the government ensured that the efforts of the country's scientists were coordinated and targeted.

On his return to Canada, Thode reported that Kapitza was not "completely happy with his lot." He was starved for visitors and "considered it a pleasure and honour to talk to foreign scientists." Thode did recall an occasion in Kapitza's office when the Russian set about testing the padding and looking for secret microphones before he spoke. On another occasion, Kapitza shared with Thode an anecdote about the great Russian nuclear physicist Andrei Sakharov. Sakharov, he related, was pleading with his fellow academicians not to carry out further nuclear tests in the atmosphere. Kapitza was standing next to Khrushchev as Sakharov made his plea. "Who is this man?" the Soviet leader asked peevishly. "He is Sakharov, father of the Soviet H-bomb and a hero of the Soviet workers," Kapitza said. Khrushchev hissed back, "You tell him to stick to his science and leave political matters to the politicians."

*Harry Thode in wheat field at his Sovereign, Saskatchewan farm (1962)*

*Harry Thode and sons with combine at Selkirk farm (1959)*

*A collage of photos from the official opening of the McMaster University Nuclear Reactor (April 1959)*

# Chapter Nine

# Thode Becomes
# President of McMaster

As principal of Hamilton College, Thode had been assuming a growing roster of responsibilities. Between 1956 and 1957, the university underwent the major reorganization that turned the former Baptist institution into a full-fledged independent university. The administration was engaged in engineering a changeover in the university's charter that would lead to the separate incorporation of the divinity school as part of the university and the creation of a non-denominational corporation to take care of the management and financing of all other parts of the university's work.

The legal integration raised the question as to whether Hamilton College should be maintained in its current form as a non-denominational affiliate of McMaster. In a memo to President Gilmour in February 1957, Thode argued that, owing to its progress and reputation, Hamilton College should continue to preserve its separate identity: "The progress we have made in Science at this University, the excellent staff we have built up, and the excellent co-operation that exists between the Science departments is, I believe, due in no small measure to the overall planning which has been possible." Thode noted that the trend was toward closer integration of the various fields of science, both pure and applied. In Hamilton College, he said, some headway had already been made toward breaking down the barriers among disciplines. "For example, in the Department of Medical Research we have induced physicists, chemists, biologists, and medical doctors to work side by side. This type of cooperation is rare in other institutions and is something that people from the outside marvel at."

As part of the reorganization plan, the university was creating the new position of vice-president. Thode was the obvious choice, but, in the same memorandum to Gilmour, he made it clear he was not interested in being promoted to this position as it was currently being presented. Stating that, while such titles as dean and principal had conventional meanings, with well-known responsibilities attached, "the position of vice-president is vague and has little or no meaning unless the duties and responsibilities are given. I therefore do not feel that I can accept the position of vice-president of McMaster University if it is offered to me unless such duties and responsibilities are officially recognized and made known."

Thode said that, as vice-president, he would want control of staff appointments, promotions, salaries, and budgets. He also wanted to preserve his control over the direction of the science program that he currently enjoyed as principal of Hamilton College. It is evident from the memo that he feared that opponents were plotting against him and trying to have his powers reduced. He even suggested he would resign if he were pushed to accept a vice-presidency that was ill-defined. "If it is felt that my duties and responsibilities should be lessened and that my powers should be curbed, then I can only assume that I no longer have the confidence or command the respect of the president and the board." The memo reveals a proud and ambitious Harry Thode, qualities that were often masked by his more public modesty and reserve.

Throughout the memo, which was practically an ultimatum, are suggestions that Thode felt unappreciated. He made reference to several organizational charts, attempts at rearranging the administrative structure of the university, which, he said, had been passed around by Herb Armstrong, dean of arts and science, and Arthur Patrick, associate dean of arts and science. Thode appeared to sense a challenge to his position. "The charts I have seen omit completely the Hamilton College picture and do not take into account the fact that I have been principal of Hamilton College for eight years. I do not believe we can turn back the clock eight or nine years and completely ignore the history of the science departments during that period and my part in it." The present administrative system, as he saw it, was working well and did not require significant change, or any lessening of his own power. "We need, of course, all the assistance we can get from the deans of faculties and chairmen of departments to work out the total requirements and the best possible distribution. However, in the final analysis, some one person must familiarize himself with all the aspects of the situation and with a small group strike a budget. To date, all matters connected with budgets, research grants, summer stipends, have come under my supervision." He went on to say that he fully realized that deans have important contributions to make and that Dean Armstrong should be more often brought in on staff matters and budget problems.

Thode eventually did take the position of vice-president, satisfied that the terms of the job would not lead to a diminution of his powers. By 1959, George Gilmour's health was failing and Thode was assuming more and more responsibilities for the running of the institution. Thode's major international reputation, and the coup he scored by bringing a nuclear reactor to McMaster, seemed to make him the heir apparent to succeed Gilmour as president.

Herb Armstrong, a geologist who had joined the faculty in 1941, had support for his presidential ambitions. He had been appointed to several decanal posts: assistant dean of arts and science (1947); associate dean of University College (1949); acting dean of arts and science (1950); dean of arts and science (1951). He held the last of these positions until he left McMaster to become vice-president at the University of Alberta, from where he moved to become the first president of the University of Calgary. Armstrong was viewed by some as more of a traditionalist than Thode, and had warned against McMaster's moving too quickly into granting doctoral degrees. Sometimes a stick-in-the-mud, Armstrong complained about students placing too much importance on athletics and the hoodlum-like behaviour that accompanied football weekends. A highly competent administrator and sound academic, if not an imaginative leader, Armstrong had won favour with Gilmour and did not hide his ambition.

Most science faculty members assumed that Thode would be the new president, but there was no such consensus in the arts and humanities, as Harry Duckworth, a top physicist at the university and close ally of Thode, found out. "People were talking about [other] possible candidates as if they were serious candidates and I was astonished that it wasn't assumed everywhere that Harry would be the president." Some people in non-science parts of the university were unaware of Thode's high international stature. Others placed relatively less value on it than scientists tended to. As well, recalls Duckworth, "there was a certain amount of resentment on the other side of the campus that Harry had pushed the science work so hard and it was requiring them to raise their research consciousness." The standard set by Thode meant more pressure on everyone else. "Although they were comfortable in directing masters" theses, if Ph.D. work were established, they would have to hang around in the summer, looking after students, which wasn't the sort of life they had entered university work to enjoy." Against Duckworth's obvious bias can be set the fact that arts faculty members who were serious about scholarship counted on summer freedom from teaching in order to do their research, knowing that doctoral students in their disciplines were less directly helpful to a professor's own research than in most science disciplines, with their laboratories, research teams, and multiple authorships of research findings.

The arts, says Duckworth, were "a blind spot" for Thode. "Thode never tried to present himself as a renaissance man. . . . He didn't have the knowledge or the natural interest." Even so, as his son Pat reports, he was interested in music. He attended concerts and recitals willingly, and he listened with rapt attention. He learned to play the flute and the piccolo, and, marginally, the piano and the recorder. He also established relations of mutual respect with committed arts scholars on campus.

When Gilmour took a leave of absence, owing to illness, for more than a year in 1960-1961, Thode was appointed acting president. It was clear then that any dissension about the presidency had not translated into a wave of support for Armstrong. Gilmour passed away in early 1961. In June, the senate and the board of governors unanimously conferred the presidency on Thode. Two other universities, McGill and Washington University of St. Louis, had been courting him for their presidential offices, but he had declined their overtures. He had devoted 22 years to McMaster, and now he was being given the opportunity to take further dramatic steps toward making it one of the finest universities in the country.

While he made sure he was offered the position, Thode still had some hesitation in accepting it. However dedicated he was to McMaster's future, his first love was research. But ambition and a concern that if he did not take the presidency someone else might lead the university in a different direction were decisive. With Whidden and Gilmour, Thode had been able to sell his expansionist vision; with Armstrong or someone else at the helm, there were no such assurances. Martin Johns recalls Thode's debating the pros and cons of the job when the two were at a conference in Oxford. Finally, through negotiations with the senate and board of governors, Thode succeeded in securing a commitment for a research assistant, which would permit him to feel confident that his research would proceed.

On the occasion of his installation, Thode quoted Sara Gibson Blanding, president of Vassar College, on the qualities a university president should have: "He must bring to his job at least an iron constitution, a zest for living, a certain flair for organization, a certain competence for dealing with and choosing people, a vision of the importance of the curriculum in relation to the sum total of our social and educational system, a sense of humour, a complete acceptance of the fact that no one is indispensable, a safeguard against pomposity." To this list, Thode added some prerequisites of his own: responsibilities to the community and the importance of his maintaining his competence as a scholar, for his own self-respect, and so that he might continue to command the respect of his colleagues.

Thode's mother had come from Saskatoon to his inauguration, but she downplayed her reaction to his success. "You must be so proud of your son," people said to her. "I'm just as proud of my son who is a farmer," she retorted. It is small wonder Harry Thode did not flaunt his achievements.

Thode took the opportunity to look toward the future, telling his audience that the scientific revolution was in full swing and his generation was experiencing an explosion of knowledge. "The problems that need to be solved are becoming more complex and everyone, including industry, government, and universities, are [sic] clamouring for the very top talent at the highest possible level. To satisfy this demand, universities must take in more students and take them to a higher level." Graduate students were not increasing in number at the desired rate, and a more serious problem, Thode noted, was the shortage of qualified people for teaching and research in the universities themselves. The requirements for exploding enrolments might not be met. "In the end we must, in effect, lift ourselves up by our bootstraps. We must train and develop these top teachers and scholars in our own halls of learning. To lower our standards and sacrifice quality for quantity would be tantamount to the admission of defeat."

Not surprisingly, he devoted a good portion of his installation address to the importance of research, saying that the best undergraduate teaching could only be done in a research environment where the spirit of inquiry prevailed. Students must be led to the frontiers between the known and the unknown, by scholars who themselves work at that frontier. He made reference to the system in the Soviet Union in which basic research was carried out in institutes established by the Soviet Academy of Sciences, leaving universities to act chiefly as teaching institutions. This could not be allowed to happen in Canada, Thode warned. Such independent institutes would drain the most valuable talent from the universities and deprive students of contacts with the most outstanding scholars.

He waded into the touchy area of what some saw as the schism between the arts and sciences. "I believe that there is really only one culture and that the idea of a conflict is a silly notion. I can do no better than to quote Albert Einstein: 'All religions, arts, and sciences are branches of the same tree. All these aspirations are directed toward ennobling man's life, lifting it from the sphere of mere physical existence, and leading the individual toward freedom.'"

The explosion of information meant that no longer could there be an Aristotle or a Leonardo who sought to master the world's entire body of knowledge. " Lest we become paralyzed by the sheer mass of knowledge, careful thought should be given to the questions, What to learn? When to learn? And, how to learn?" "On the other hand," Thode warned, "No man can be considered cultured who is in complete ignorance of a whole field of human endeavour. It will be our aim to strive for a truly liberal education in which science is taught in relation to the other disciplines and in which the human-ities are infused with science."

Perhaps it was his own role, however small, in the creation of the atomic bomb that led him to conclude on a worried note. "Man has the power of destroying natural life around him on an unprecedented scale. We need to be guided from the greatest tragedy man can know. All the best that has been written in the name of art, religion, and history, all the great experiences of man must be called upon to save us from tragedy. The problems confronting us are most complex and must be solved both on the intellectual level and on the emotional level. What is needed is a new order of ethical and social responsibility."

Thode wondered aloud whether Canadians would be able to share in the new exciting scientific discoveries of the future or if these would pass the country by. He worried that the nation's politicians might fail to recognize how much of Canada's wealth would depend on the application of science to industry. He lamented the beliefs in some government circles that education cost too much and that research and scholarly work were a luxury Canadians could not afford. He called for another $1 billion to be spent on higher education and university and government research. In the race for commercial atomic power, Canada, he said, could be leading the way, but there was little appre-ciation of the pioneering research, of which he was a big part, that had gone on in Canada since 1939. Many people, he lamented, were still confused even about the definition of a scientist. "When they think of the advances in science they think of the benefits of science in terms of material comforts, not of the great scientific discoveries themselves. Perhaps worst of all, they do not realize that material comforts and productivity are just by-products of scientific knowledge and understanding."

# Chapter Ten

# McMaster's Strength in Science, Oppenheimer's Whidden Lectures

Thode took over the presidency with a strong administrative and academic team. He had an unerring eye for talent and, through the years, had helped, if not in recruiting, then in bringing to prominence such distinguished scientists as Arthur Bourns, Harry Duckworth, Howard Petch, Mel Preston, Richard Tomlinson, and others. In the arts, the strong scholars included Togo Salmon, Roy Wiles, Bert McCready, Craig McIvor, Alexander McKay, and others, with whom Thode, now as president, would be working. In addition, in arts, science, and engineering, increasingly large numbers of able young academics were beginning their careers at McMaster and, by sheer numbers and the diversity of their academic interests, were beginning to weaken the oligarchic patterns of administration that, until now, had prevailed. In 1961, Bourns, then dean of the faculty of graduate studies, wanted to return to research and to the classroom. Thode, while envisioning greater administrative roles for Bourns in the future, acceded to this wish. Harry Duckworth, who had worked on Thode's wartime team, and then left McMaster only to return to build the physics department, took over the leadership of the graduate faculty.

Howard Petch and Harry Thode had become close partners in research, and, when Thode assumed the presidency, he relinquished his position of director of research and turned it over to Petch. Petch had joined the McMaster faculty in 1954, after taking his Ph.D. at the University of British Columbia and doing postdoctoral studies at McMaster and further research as a Rutherford fellow at Cambridge. In these early years, Petch appreciated the Thode style from their first meeting. "I was working in the lab and this fellow [Thode] came in and drew up a stool. He sat there, it must have been nearly an hour, talking about what I was doing. Even though we didn't know him, he was sort of an inspiration because everybody talked in whispered terms about what he was doing."

Thode spotted exceptional talent in Petch and encouraged him to help set up a program in metallurgy, which Stelco and Dofasco wanted at McMaster. Thode got Mike Hedden to do most of the paperwork for Petch in preparing a draft curriculum for the new program. Thode then started interviewing for a possible chairman. A couple of highly recommended candidates Thode had in mind were traditional physical metallurgists, recalls Petch. Typically, Thode wanted someone with a more innovative edge, and he rejected the traditionalists in favour of an untried candidate, Petch himself. "It was," says Petch, "a great surprise to me and a great gamble on his part. I thought about it and finally said I would make a bargain with him. I would become chair and develop the department, if he would let me use that as the core around which to build a materials research institute." Thode agreed.

Once Thode spotted talent he was prepared to go beyond bureaucratic and institutional boundaries to see that the talent flourished. "Everything was done to help you get your research started," Petch recalls. Even though there were much more senior people around, Thode would always be looking to the young minds. Petch says he had never dreamed of doing administrative work, for example, but Thode was prepared to overlook his inexperience.

Petch also appreciated Thode's informality. He remembers Thode taking the trouble of going by overnight train with him to Ottawa to meet with the Defence Research Board to help get financial support for Petch to hire a professor in solid state physics. "We went by train, came back by train. I'll never forget, we got this tiny little double room in the Chateau Laurier, way up on the top floor. Harry had brought a Spy apple, a large Spy apple, and I'll never forget him flopping down on his bed, grabbing this apple, which he just twisted and split in half and threw me half."

Mike Hedden had worked for many years as assistant to Thode and as assistant director of research. He had been closely associated with the development, construction, and organization of the McMaster nuclear reactor program and the engineering program. He was now appointed the university's business administrator, which, given his skills, became a major source of power and influence.

Thode had a formidable science team and a big reputation in scientific circles, but he was not without his weaknesses. He was not strong in the arts, having little personal interest in that part of the intellectual world, although he was often a receptive and ready listener for arts faculty members when they talked to him of their research work and aspirations. From the arts and humanities parts of the campus, it was natural that a science man would face suspicion in taking over the presidency. In Thode's case, the situation was exacerbated by the fact that he had placed virtually all his energies in the science areas of McMaster. He had charted the course and, with Gilmour, brought the university from a theological base to a secular one. This had made possible government funding and serious development of science.

Most of Thode's colleagues knew he was not strong on administrative detail and that he would find this aspect of the job uncongenial. Nor was he good on a public platform. In Gilmour, the university had a wonderful public presence, the quintessential university cardinal, a man who looked the part, who was authoritative, spoke in eloquent cadences, and could command attention. Thode's self-effacement was a liability at a time when the new medium of television was beginning to place a premium on personal charisma. Sadie Thode told her husband, "You're not George Gilmour and don't try to be."

If he did not have Gilmour's charisma, Thode had a warmth the former president lacked. While Gilmour was a formal and sometimes intimidating presence, Thode was entirely approachable. He had, of course, an academic standing that Gilmour never enjoyed. In some ways he was a more modern man, free of the prudishness and shirt-and-tie rigour of his predecessor. Modes of dress and behaviour were rapidly becoming less formal and Thode was part of this social change. With him as president, faculty members would now be able to enjoy a drink without looking over their shoulders. Thode enjoyed recounting the occasion when he was vice-president and Gilmour was hosting a Soviet delegation. The Soviets, Gilmour knew, were big on alcoholic libations, and he had no choice but to set aside a table of booze in a corner of the meeting room. Not wanting to be seen in that corner with his hard-drinking guests, Gilmour instructed Thode to handle bartending duties. It was as if to say, "You, Harry, are sufficiently reprobate in this regard to handle such a duty." In recounting the story, Thode would say, "I know why he made me vice-president. I was vice-president of vice."

Thode's administrative team was strong, and conflicting ambitions were bound to cause conflict. Some detected friction between Duckworth and Thode, because Duckworth had the capacity to be a president himself. Petch, most knew, also harboured such goals. He was an ambitious man, a man in a hurry, a man who, recalls Martin Johns, "wasn't very good at personal relationships, particularly at the beginning."

On Thode's ascendancy, the university was in full expansion. Four new buildings had just opened. These were the student centre, which took the name Wentworth House, an arts and administration building named Gilmour Hall, and two new student residences, Moulton Hall and Whidden Hall. These buildings marked the end of a four-year physical expansion program costing $12 million. Plans for another expansion phase at a cost of $9 million were on the books. This would include a physical education centre, general sciences and earth sciences buildings, a lecture hall addition to the arts and administration building, additions to both the arts and science libraries, and extensive renovations to University Hall and Hamilton Hall.

There was more of everything, more buildings, more students, more research, more money. The university's operating budget was $4 million, with revenues almost enough to balance the books. Government grants brought in $1.5 million, student fees accounted for just over $1 million, endowments brought $134,000, and research grants another $675,000. Sundry items helped boost the total.

Enrollment for full-time students was fewer than two thousand for 1961-1962, but was projected to balloon to seven thousand full-time day students by the 1970-1971 academic year. Large numbers of students were in extension degree and non-degree courses. Faculty members totalled 175 professors and lecturers. Enrolling did not come cheap. The minimum student fee was $465, which was as high as the fee at any other university in the country. Tuition plus residence cost $1,090. Thode was interested in excellence more than economy. Visiting the University of British Columbia in 1960, he advised students, perhaps thinking of the time he left the high-paying chemical company in New Jersey for a much reduced salary at McMaster, to "select a job you like, plan to get good experience and make the best contribution you can." Certainly, he added, "the initial salary should be secondary."

His practical sense extended to university admissions. Thode did not like the trend that saw only grade 13 examination results as the criteria for admission to university. "By continuing to require higher and higher performance in such exams," he said, "we will soon reach the level where we cut out some of our most imaginative people, students who perhaps are non-conformists but, once they find themselves, will leave many of the others far behind. I can think of Churchill and Einstein as examples."

Influenced by his education on the prairies where there was no grade 13, Thode wanted it abolished in Ontario. An Ontario Ministry of Education committee recommended this in 1964 and Thode heartily endorsed this. "I have felt for a long time that five years was too long for most students to spend in a high school environment and that they could be prepared and ready for post-secondary education after four years of high school, whether it be in a university, a community college, or a technical institute. Furthermore it seems ridiculous that we in Ontario with our 13 grades of primary and secondary school should be an island of isolation in this continent, making it more difficult for the exchange of students between Ontario and other provinces and between Ontario and the United States." Thode's position may have been far-sighted. Certainly it was shared by quite a number of people in the expansionist period of the universities, when first-year admission requirements were loosening and subjects like foreign languages were being discarded for entrance to many university programs, and so were doomed in most schools as well. But grade 13 is to remain in the Ontario curriculum until 2003.

Thode was also an early proponent of community colleges, stating his disappointment that the committee did not recommend any specific action in this regard. Such colleges, he believed, would provide a more practical type of post-secondary education in the fields of technology and the applied arts.

In keeping with its effort to establish a leading reputation in the sciences, McMaster became, in 1961, the first university to use computers to compile examination and course timetables. With computers—not without many glitches and considerable staff and student frustration—McMaster was boiling down six weeks of work by the registrar and his staff to about two weeks by International Business Machines.

Thode saw McMaster's expansion as key to the future of Hamilton. In 1962, he told area businessmen that "the importance of the universities in the whole national research complex is now being recognized by financiers and real estate firms." In order to attract wealth, a city had to have a pleasant environment and a great university. "Many hundreds of industries in recent years have chosen to locate near the Massachusetts Institute of Technology and Harvard, on the one hand, and the California Institute of Technology and the University of California, on the other." He quoted a study which disclosed that MIT alumni had established 75 new industries in Boston since the close of the war. He had big visions and knew he would need the backing of city hall and of industry. He put his salesman's hat on, confident that the same formula that worked in Boston and California could work in Hamilton. "The important thing is that we have a great university. We must attract the best staff, provide the best facilities and support a first-class graduate program. This is our aim at McMaster," he told those in the community who were in a position to further his goals.

At the same time as he was touting the American institutions, Thode was lobbying against a proposal to create a technical institute like the Massachusetts Institute of Technology (MIT) in Canada. The idea was put forward by J.B. Warren, a professor of physics at the University of British Columbia. He wanted to base a Canadian Institute of Technology on the model of the California Institute of Technology. These American institutions offered high standards, high-calibre staff, a high staff-student ratio, and an administration solely concerned with research planning and the training of scientists and engineers. These were the very things, Warren argued, that Canada, with its generalist universities that tended to emphasize the liberal arts, could not provide to engineering and other technical students. A specialized institute would provide a badly needed stimulus for Canadian research and a more flexible approach to science. It would retain the best minds within Canadian borders, rather than see them flee south of the border. Warren said his proposal should be a project for Canada's 1967 centennial year.

Thode was an admirer of MIT and Cal Tech and knew that the system of institutes in the Soviet Union was the basis for that country's advanced reputation in science. But he opposed Warren's plan for several reasons, the strongest being that he did not want to see the McMaster he was building taking second seat in science to such an institution. He agreed with Bourns's argument against the Warren proposal that, at this stage of Canada's development, the creation of a super-institution for research and training in science and engineering could only weaken these activities in existing universities like McMaster. It would drain off the best and the brightest faculty, their most promising graduate students, and essential research funds.

Thode did not want this competition, nor did he welcome new universities with graduate programs that might draw resources from his own. In correspondence with the National Research Council, he regretted the proliferation of universities in Ontario intent on establishing graduate programs. He pointed out that in California extensive Ph.D. work was limited to five or six big universities and that the thirty or so state senior colleges were not permitted to do graduate work. "It seems to be a fact that most of the doctorates in the U.S. come from a few of the top graduate schools and . . . this situation can be expected to continue. . . . Maybe I am unduly concerned, but I would not like to see 10 to 12 institutions, in Ontario, all with second-class graduate schools."

Thode also noted that a Cal Tech of Canada would not solve the problem of the failure of many Canadian industries to pursue research at home. Most Canadian subsidiaries, Thode observed, continued to rely on basic research done in the U.S., and many Canadian graduates were going there. Thode and Bourns thought the solution lay in the creation across Canada of first-rate technical community colleges into which could be directed about half the number of students finding their way into universities. With such a public policy, the universities could better concentrate their resources, even though the large facts of a branch-plant economy with minimum corporate commitment to research in Canada would still remain.

Thode made clear his remarkable ambitions for McMaster in a letter sent to Ontario Minister of Labour Bill Warrender. "McMaster University," he wrote, "has an opportunity to become one of the great universities of this continent." He told Warrender the time had come for a preparation of a master plan for McMaster because "we are, I believe, at the crossroads." Continued growth would require more lands. He was eyeing the part of the Royal Botanical Gardens which sat just south of the campus. He was making appeals to governments for more funds, particularly for science research. In a letter to the National Research Council he argued that "Canadian science is coming of age, and much greater support is required in the future. The expansion of university science is a precursor to the expansion of applied research and industrial development work."

Thode was in office only a few months when he brought a figure of world renown to the campus. In 1962, Dr. J. Robert Oppenheimer, the father of the A-bomb, appeared at McMaster to give the annual Whidden lectures. Thode, along with his predecessor Gilmour, had invited Oppenheimer, then director of the Institute for Advanced Study in Princeton. No reply came at first, and Thode grew frustrated. He then met Oppenheimer at celebrations marking the hundredth anniversary of the founding of MIT. When Thode raised the matter of the invitation, Oppenheimer apologized for not responding, explaining that his work load was great and that he had another concern: the McMaster invitation included the requirement that the lectures be published in book form. Oppenheimer felt he lacked the time to take on such a task. Thode assured him he would get a top physicist to edit the lectures for publication, and Oppenheimer was then persuaded to accept the invitation.

Thode's invitation to Oppenhemier was thought to be a brave move by some at McMaster. After the deployment of atomic weapons against Japan, the American physicist had become an outspoken proponent of civilian and international control of atomic energy. When he opposed the development of the hydrogen bomb in 1949, on both technical and moral grounds, he was suspended from his position at the Atomic Energy Commission as a potential security risk. This move aroused strong controversy, but Oppenheimer was eventually exonerated and re-elected to his position as director of Princeton's Institute for Advanced Study.

So great was the demand for tickets for the lectures by Oppenheimer that the location had to be moved to the Drill Hall, where 1800 people could be seated. The eminent and controversial nuclear scientist gave highly technical talks, well over the heads of most lay people. "But he had a bedside manner," recalls Duckworth, one of the professors who introduced him, "and he said things in such a way that you thought you understood them." During his lectures Oppenheimer paced the front of the hall. He had a stack of papers in his hand and on each page were three or four words written in very large letters. When finished with one page he would toss it to the floor and move on to the next with the flourish of an actor.

He touched on a range of topics related to the responsibilities of scientists around the world. His philosophy mirrored Thode's. "The deep things in science were found not because they were useful, but because it was possible to find them," said Oppenheimer. He rejected the idea that the scientists who created the atomic bomb were irresponsible. "You don't sit in front of an insoluble problem forever," he commented. "In the end, you are guided by . . . what it is possible to learn."

In his final lecture he reflected on the dropping of the bombs on Hiroshima and Nagasaki. He was convinced, he said, that the war would likely have been drawn out without them and would quite possibly have cost more lives. Nevertheless, his own feeling was that, if the bombs were to be used, there could have been more effective warning and less wanton killing than actually took place in the heat of battle and the confusion of the campaign. When the war was over, he noted, "The great men of physics spoke quite simply and eloquently, Einstein in advocacy of world government and Bohr, first to Roosevelt and to Churchill and to General Marshall . . . of the need to work for a world which was completely open." This vision of a scientific world that operated openly and with cooperation was one Thode clearly shared.

Finally, Oppenheimer quoted to applause a passage from a top secret report on the bomb. "If this weapon does not persuade men of the need for international collaboration and the need to put an end to war, nothing that comes out of a laboratory ever will."

During the visit the world's preeminent nuclear scientist spent an evening at the president's house, impressing everyone with his extreme politeness. Whenever Sadie rose to leave the room, he stood up. Whenever she returned, he stood up again. She came away an admirer of Oppenheimer's gentility, politesse, and mastery of the language. She later said that she felt he had the soul of a poet, an intriguing characteristic for the father of the A-bomb. Thode also proudly took Oppenheimer on a tour of McMaster's nuclear reactor, during which he noticed Oppenheimer's fascination with the bright glow of the nuclear fire in the pool of the reactor.

Oppenhemier had told an interviewer of the words from Hindu scripture that had crossed his mind when the first A-bomb had detonated: "I am become death, the shatterer of worlds . . . ." He said that he now wished that no country possessed the weapons that had resulted from his work, and praised Canada for demonstrating "political balance by not owning nuclear weapons. There is already too much danger from the arms race." The fact that nothing had happened in the 16 years since the first atomic bomb was dropped "makes one hopeful of the chances that there will be no nuclear war," he added. A few weeks after the visit, Thode conscripted Mel Preston to edit the transcriptions of Oppenheimer's lectures into a book which, like other Whidden Lectures, was published by Oxford University Press.

Thode came close to leaving McMaster in 1962, when he was seriously considered as a successor to E.W.R. Steacie, the longtime president of the National Research Council. Thode, who had been getting grants from the N.R.C. ever since he arrived at McMaster, had formed a close alliance with Steacie. Steacie grew seriously ill and died suddenly in 1962 after returning from a vacation in his lakeside cottage in the Gatineau hills north of Ottawa. It was known that Steacie favoured Thode as his successor. Thode later told friends that, had he been able to see Steacie before he died, he probably would have felt an obligation to accept the job. When the time came to choose a new president of the National Research Council, Prime Minister John Diefenbaker did offer the position to Thode, but he turned it down. He was not ready to abandon McMaster so early in his presidency, but his admiration for Steacie and his high regard for the importance of the work of the N.R.C. made the decision a difficult one. In an article written for the Royal Society of Canada, Thode expressed his views on Steacie's achievements. At the end of the 1930s, Thode noted, Canada was "a backward nation scientifically." Industrial research was almost non-existent; only two or three universities had anything resembling research programs; and government research laboratories were small and poorly supported. But by the early 1960s, Thode wrote, Canada was in the forefront of fields ranging from atomic physics to the study of structures of complex organic substances. Many scientists contributed, Thode noted, but none more than Steacie. "It was his vision, judgement and leadership which gave the whole development direction and impetus."

Among the things for which Thode praised Steacie were policies Thode himself favoured. One was the need to increase support for scientific research at universities. Another was his forceful opposition, as Thode put it, "to the extreme measures of secrecy which were introduced to scientific affairs during the war in the name of national security." It was Steacie's view, he noted, that the secrecy and complete isolation of scientists from other colleagues in other areas could only hinder scientific progress. Steacie could be congratulated, Thode said, for spearheading Canadian-Soviet scientific exchanges.

Because of his own glowing reputation, Thode's advice was sought on a wide range of subjects by universities across Canada. John Saywell, associate dean of arts and science at Toronto's fledgling York University (founded in 1959), asked for Thode's recommendations for chairman of the chemistry department. Thode responded with a list of seven names, providing curt reviews of each and imparting his own preferences. Of a candidate from Ottawa, Thode wrote, "a bit of a prima donna who is mainly interested in furthering his own reputation." Thode found the research record of a candidate from the Royal

Military College lacking, and pointed to a lecture the man had given on the teaching of organic chemistry which, Thode said, was not impressive. As for a leading candidate from McGill, Thode thought highly of his abilities as a chemist and his research record but had other reservations. "He is aggressive and would perhaps get things done. However, I am concerned about his ability to deal with people. Whereas he might do well as a chairman of the chemistry department, I am wondering whether he would be diplomatic enough to give leadership in the broad area of science."

Thode's comments came down to an appreciation of good judgment as the key to the development and administration of a complex institution like a university. McMaster was to prosper under Thode's leadership largely because he possessed this elusive and valuable quantity in rare abundance, and the times were with him.

*R. H. Tomlinson (April 1960)*

# Chapter Eleven

# The Founding of the McMaster Faculty of Health Sciences

Thode had begun thinking of the possibility of a medical school for McMaster in 1949, but at that time many factors weighed against any immediate planning. McMaster was still a small liberal arts institution and, for "a colossal undertaking" such as a medical school, the university first had to build a strong base in the sciences, Thode believed. The creation of Hamilton College was a route to achieving this goal, especially because the college's independent status now made it eligible for government grants not permitted by the university's base in a religious denomination.

Thode's creation, in 1948, of a department of medical research to investigate the use of radioisotopes in the diagnosis and treatment of disease was an initial step toward what was to become a faculty of health sciences, including but not restricted, scientifically or professionally, to a school of medicine. The work at McMaster, done in a war-surplus H hut, included the treatment of patients referred by Hamilton doctors for radioactive procedures, which eventually led to the creation of radioisotope labs at two Hamilton hospitals. McMaster biochemist Samuel Kirkwood, whose work in diagnosing thyroid disorders with radioiodine led to significant discoveries pertaining to enzymes in the thyroid, became so sought-after that Thode lost him to the University of Minnesota. Further misfortune struck the lab with the death of Charles Jaimet, the first director of McMaster's radioisotope clinic, in 1963. His friend's death was a terrible blow for Thode, who had looked forward to Jaimet's playing a major role in the expansion of McMaster.

Throughout the 1950s, discussion of the advisability of creating a medical school at McMaster had grown. In 1953, in a memo to president Gilmour, Thode recommended that land be set aside for a university hospital, but, at the time, university lands were considered insufficient for existing development plans, let alone a medical school. Many doctors in the city had become keen to see a school built, inspired in part by the apparent success of the medical research unit. In 1956, Sir Frances Fraser, who headed the postgraduate school of medicine in London, England, came to deliver the Redman lectures on the subject of medical education. Thode invited him to explore the possibility of a medical school for McMaster. Fraser visited the medical schools in Ontario to ascertain whether another one was needed. "We felt very strongly," recalled Thode, "that unless there was a real need, we weren't going to get the funds to build a really first-class medical school, and we insisted from the beginning that there were enough second-class medical schools in North America without building another one." Hamilton, at that time, was the largest urban area in the country to lack such a facility.

Fraser concluded there was no immediate urgency, but that in seven or eight years there would be. The Ontario government, meanwhile, was starting to hear proposals for medical schools from other universities, including Windsor and Laurentian in Sudbury. Premier Leslie Frost let it be known he would like to have a proposal from McMaster. Thode was aware of the enormous costs of entering into such a venture and was interested only if the province would bear a major portion of the financial burden. He also told Frost that McMaster was committed to building a first-class medical school that would have to include an integrated university hospital.

At this time, the future of the Hamilton Sanatorium, which had once been the largest tuberculosis hospital in the British Empire, was being debated. Located on Hamilton Mountain and seven miles from McMaster, this now underused facility was mentioned as a possible site for a university hospital and medical school. The administration saw disadvantages to having the school located off-campus, but were impressed by the cost-saving possibilities of using an existing structure.

Talks continued in Thode's first two years as president. In October 1963, he presented a brief to newly elected premier John Robarts for a school costing an estimated $24 million, and incorporating a 360-bed teaching hospital that would also train nurses, therapists, and medical technologists. Thode's brief came with sound arguments for McMaster's selection over other university sites, citing community support, the existence of Canada's first nuclear reactor, and the presence of a department of medical research. One year after the submission of the brief, McMaster was awarded the project.

As a nuclear physicist, Thode was no expert on how to set up a medical school but, ever the conscientious student, he prepared by reading reports and books on the history of leading American medical schools. He visited the medical school at the University of Florida in Gainesville and consulted with administrators at Harvard, who advised him to locate both the school and the teaching hospital on the campus. Harvard's own medical school and hospital are located apart, in Cambridge and Boston.

To follow the on-campus model, space was a prime concern. With some foresight Thode had already begun proceedings to acquire land from the Royal Botanical Gardens, which were jointly owned by Ontario's Department of Highways, the Parks Board of the City of Hamilton, and the university. In 1963 these negotiations were completed, with the transfer of 1,309 acres of Royal Botanical Gardens land to the university.

In the same year, Thode brought in a landscape architect to advise on the development of the campus. He could not find an appropriate Canadian for the job and so settled on a Japanese-American, Hideo Sasaki, of Sasaki, Walker and Associates in Watertown, Massachusetts. Sasaki had experience designing for prestigious universities in the United States and was a professor of landscape architecture at Harvard. Some at McMaster thought that these credentials impressed Thode to an excessive degree.

Sasaki submitted a plan for an integrated campus, with the medical centre on the RBG site bordered to the south by Main Street. A stranger to the Steel City, he had little sense of the deep attachment of Hamiltonians to the Gardens. Though he was acquiring additional lands with the RBG transfer, Thode had initially thought of other possible locations for the new school. "In planning the site," recalled Thode, "we had thought the medical school should be back of the Physical Education Centre. There is a big field back in there and we already got an easement from the city to put a road back there." Sasaki's plan would mean streets would have to be closed off and a major artery, King Street, rerouted. His view was that the hospital had to be on the periphery of campus interfacing with the city, so that patients could be brought directly in rather than taken to a building behind the campus. Thode and his colleagues did not ask many questions. Had they known the costs and the headaches Sasaki's plan would ultimately engender, they might have been more critical. When sites other than the one using King Street were suggested to Sasaki, he would  not listen: "If you insist, I will resign from the job," Thode quoted Sasaki as saying, suggesting the architect was forcing his hand. But at the same time, Thode seemed to think Sasaki's arguments made good sense. In another interview, he said, "These things sounded all very reasonable to me." Once Thode's mind was made up, it was rare for it to be changed. Sasaki's point of view quickly became his own.

Government authorities were not prepared to go ahead with financing unless the university could assure them of arrangements for additional lands for future expansion. Their reasoning was based on the problems they had had with other universities and their exorbitant costs in acquiring, on short notice, lands for expansion. McMaster, therefore, proposed to expropriate residential properties immediately to the east of the proposed site. It would purchase 87 of these properties, giving occupants the option of selling outright or selling and leasing back their properties from the university for 15 years.

The news of the expropriation plan sparked an outcry in the university and in the city of Hamilton. Some of Thode's closest supporters on campus deserted him. One was Harry Duckworth: "He wanted to get residents of Westdale out to a council meeting," Duckworth recalls. "I refused to go." Duckworth could scarcely believe that an important part of the beautiful Royal Botanical Gardens would be torn down while other sites were being so readily overlooked. "To destroy the Gardens and replace them with an oil refinery was just a terrible thing," Duckworth said, years after the health sciences complex was built, showing his dismay at what many saw as the project's overly utilitarian design.

Faculty members in both the sciences and the arts expressed concern that the giant construction, including a hospital, would overshadow the rest of the university, leaving all other faculties to take a back seat. They feared that McMaster would become a "mediversity." Many favoured locating the complex well off campus, hoping thereby to reduce its impact.

Another line of thought suggested that the new institution should consist of smaller educational and service units spread throughout the city in order to respond more directly to citizens' needs. This idea found some support among medical experts at the campus, including William Spaulding, who wrote a book about the centre: "A health sciences centre reinforced the notion," he wrote, "that the health services establishment was remote from the people in need. Students should not be educated in the 'ivory tower' environment of a massive building on campus, because nothing should be interposed between the students and the down-to-earth problems of people in the community."

As the controversy mounted, a compromise solution gained favour. Across the four-lane highway Cootes Drive, west toward Dundas, McMaster owned land that might be suitable for the building. Arthur Bourns was among those who suggested the site to Thode, recommending a tunnel be constructed under the highway to connect the school to the campus. Thode responded with a cold rebuke that shocked Bourns. To Thode's eventual relief, it was determined that the soft and swampy soil conditions in the area would require deep supporting piles to be constructed, thus bringing on exorbitant costs.

Everyone who challenged Thode's vision for the health sciences centre met the same obstinacy. When questioned by opponents, he was unmoveable. "It has to be on campus," he said flatly. "A modern medical school has to be integrated with the sciences and social sciences. If they are separated it will be just impossible. If it has to be up at the Hamilton Health Association, up on the mountain, then Waterloo or some other university should be building this medical school."

Sasaki's plans involving the closing of King Street, and the subsequent expropriations were accepted by McMaster without any initial public consultation or referral to Hamilton city council. In June 1963, the university invited Mayor Victor Copps and city councillors to the campus. According to reports from the session, a shocked city official asked Sasaki, "Who gave you permission to act as if King Street didn't exist?" Sasaki's response was that he had received such authorization from the university. In 1964, Mayor Copps put a request to his Board of Control to close part of King Street. It received approval, but opposition was mounting. The plan still had to be approved by a vote of the full city council, some of whom charged that the issue was being railroaded through the approval process.

At a council meeting on January 19, 1965, it looked as if the plan might go down to defeat. But Mayor Copps deftly avoided the vote by referring the matter back to committee on a technicality. Realizing the precariousness of his position, Thode came forward with new plans. Instead of diverting King Street traffic down Forsyth, McMaster would pay most of the cost of a diversion to be built on campus land and leave Forsyth Street alone. "These concessions are not easy to make," Thode explained, "as we need every bit of land we can retain. But we feel it removes what seems to be the chief objection to the extension, which is that it would cost the taxpayers a large sum of money. Under this scheme, the main part of the cost will be the responsibility of the university, leaving a maximum of $250,000 to be paid by the city."

Council was happy with the compromise and passed it unanimously. But Thode was soon to find out that he had issued the proposal too hastily. If campus land was used for the King Street extension, the proposed new buildings could not be arranged in proper relation to one another. The goal of integrating the new health sciences facilities with one another and with the rest of the campus would not be met.

Now Thode had to eat crow, disavow his own compromise, and go back to city council with another plan that was far less attractive. The university wanted the diversion to start a block east of Forsyth, at Dalewood. The proposed expropriation of some 90 homes was back on the books. Scott Young wrote in the *Globe and Mail* that this shift gave the impression of being "a brand-new land grab." Mayor Copps was not happy. "I was surprised and disappointed when McMaster came back and said they couldn't live with the expansion plan we'd agreed on after such a big fight. When you get rid of a hot potato, you'd like to see it gone," he told Young.

As 1965 progressed, more Hamiltonians became aware of the major dislocations and disruptions the mammoth new complex would cause. There were fears the traffic situation would become intolerable, that expropriation of homes would disfigure a once handsome neighbourhood, that parking would be a nightmare, and that the area would be flooded with sufferers of rare and contagious diseases. These were miserable times for Thode. He would later say that the strife took ten years off his life. The storm of protest lasted two years. Some protestors even resorted to making abusive phone calls to the Thodes' residence. Sadie fielded most of them, often late at night from unidentified callers. One told Sadie he was going to blow up the Thode home with her in it. Sadie told Harry about this call but kept quiet about many other harsh criticisms and threats, to spare him further upset.

In his long fight for the health sciences complex, Harry Thode was fortunate to have three of Hamilton's most powerful men in his corner. The first was Mayor Vic Copps, the second *Hamilton Spectator* publisher Tom Nichols, and the third Ken Soble, the proprietor of CHCH-TV and CHML Radio. "Everybody else," recalled Thode, "seemed to be against us." It helped his cause that Nichols and Soble sat on the McMaster board of governors. Nichols tried to resign once, citing the appearance of a conflict of interest, but his offer was refused.

Thode also had a vital link to powerful board member Edward Carey Fox. The McMaster alumnus, who had owned Canada Packers before going into banking and finance, had been a vital player in the university's development since the 1920s. He was a financial contributor, board member, key adviser to the president, and a conduit to industry, finance, and business. Fox had a steady hand and an enlightened appreciation of the university and its importance. Thode cultivated a warm relationship with Fox in the 1940s and gained his lasting confidence and support.

Thode's opponents included popular alderwoman Anne Jones, who represented the area affected by the proposed changes and who led the charge against the project, in spite of her personal admiration for Thode. "They saw," said Thode of the opposition, "that there was this undercurrent against this big machine, the university, just taking over the community, and they were able, for a while, to get a lot of people on their side."

Even Thode supporter Ken Soble acknowledged that the Thode camp often lacked sensitivity to the community: "You have to realize the way Harry Thode and his people felt," he told the *Globe and Mail*. "They were so pleased with themselves at accomplishing this thing that they thought everybody who heard about it would be jumping for joy, and the grateful city would rush in and do the piddling little details—such as closing a few streets," he added wryly.

In his full-page report, Scott Young concluded that "McMaster got itself into a jam primarily by a hamhanded lack of understanding of public relations. The people were kept in ignorance until a virtual fait accompli was sprung on them and an attempt made to push it into law. If McMaster had set out in detail, in 1963, its plans, hopes and aspirations, perhaps in pamphlet form available to all, the shock and surprise at the dribble of revelations in 1965 and 1966 would never have occurred."

Certain members of the McMaster faculty remained among Thode's most severe critics. Norman Shrive of the English department admired his president but found it difficult to condone the "overbearing way" in which the project was being driven. Being the man of science, says Shrive, Thode had no sense of aesthetics on the campus. "Thank God for Sadie," he laughs. At receptions having anything to do with cultural matters, Thode, in Shrive's view, was clearly out of his element. He would stand smiling silently and let Sadie carry the conversation, which she was well able to do given her interest in the arts. Others report, however, about her somewhat reticent husband in such situations, that he not infrequently made incisive comments on such things as chamber music performances, which he clearly enjoyed.

It was hard even for the critics to dislike Thode, notes Shrive. His apparent lack of ego was disarming. "You never felt that Harry was doing this [health sciences centre] for his own self-aggrandizement," says Shrive. "He was your farm boy from Saskatchewan." His approachability, his easy way with people, and his great skills at managing meetings were helpful attributes during this time of conflict. However acrimonious the debate over the health sciences centre became, few of Thode's opponents ever abandoned their respect for him.

While negotiations with the city on the site for the new faculty and hospital wore on, Thode began a search for a dean of medicine. Ray Farquharson, who had been dean of medicine at the University of Toronto and was now vice-president of the National Research Council, provided Thode with a shortlist of candidates. Thode and his colleagues interviewed them all, but Harry did not think any had the qualities necessary to build the type of institution he had in mind. He asked Farquharson for other possibilities, and was recommended an exceptionally promising young man at the University of Toronto named John Evans. Evans, who was not yet a full professor, was keenly interested in medical education and was in the process of making a survey of it in the United States and Europe.

Thode agreed to meet Evans at the King Edward Hotel in Toronto. How would he recognize Evans, Thode asked during their phone conversation. "I'll be the tallest man there," Evans replied.

Over lunch, the two men got along splendidly. "Dr. Farquharson had told me what a brilliant scientist Thode was, and what a great leader," recalls Evans. "Here was this very personal, humble individual, almost diffident in his presentation, but every time you talked about something he would press you a little bit more and a little bit more to probe your ideas. . . . He had a wonderful, gentle way of getting information. He pushed you to the limits of the knowledge you had, and I often thought, I bet it was like that being a graduate student for him, that he would take the problem you were dealing with and discuss it with you through his own style, get you to push the frontiers of your knowledge about the problem." Though impressed by Thode, Evans told him that the McMaster position did not suit him at this stage of his career: "I wasn't interested in the job at all," says Evans. "I had just got all my labs going at the University of Toronto and I was very much engaged in teaching and enjoying it enormously and looking after patients. It was all I had trained to do for about 12 years."

The following week Evans travelled to Atlantic City to deliver a paper to the Federation of American Scientists of Experimental Biology. Some thirty thousand scientists would be attending, and Evans had visions of his paper on the functioning of the heart muscle receiving an ovation from at least five thousand at his session. But when he went to the room where he was to speak there were three people: "I knew I was in the wrong room so I checked. It turned out to be the right room," he recalls ruefully. On the way home, Evans began to rethink his decision to decline Thode's offer of the deanship. He came to the conclusion that the position offered the potential to chart exciting new ground in Canadian medical education. He now scolded himself for his haste in evaluating what McMaster had to offer.

Two months passed. Thode had talked to more candidates but still had not found the right person. On a whim, he said (it had to be more than that), he decided to call Evans again to make sure he was not interested. Evans told Thode he had changed his mind, and they came to an agreement without any discussion of a precise job description or salary plans: "It wasn't a negotiation any time with Harry Thode. It really was a capture of a set of ideas that he seemed to think were reasonable and worth trying to do. . . . You just had the feeling that he would do everything in his power to overcome the inevitable obstacles you were going to encounter."

Evans came on board in July 1965, while Thode was in full turmoil with the city over the siting of the health sciences complex. All the dreams Thode had invested in Evans soon seemed achievable. Evans was energetic, enthusiastic, polite, imaginative, brilliant in negotiation, and superior at building alliances. His philosophy of medical education twinned exactly with Thode's. Both men put a high premium on research and favoured close connections between medicine and the university's other scientific disciplines. New doctors needed to keep abreast of the explosion in scientific knowledge as it applied to medical practice. Evans and Thode saw that McMaster, with its sophisticated science programs, could expand significantly the relationship between science and medicine, creating the potential for breakthroughs in diagnostics and treatment.

Thode met some resistance among the university's senate and board of governors to the appointment of a dean who had not even attained the level of associate professor, but he was eventually able to persuade them that Evans was the man for the job.

Dissent from within the campus on the ambitious project, however, still preyed. "There was resentment in the science departments," recalls physicist Carman McMullen. He remembers a faculty meeting in the council chamber when it became apparent that members of the science faculty were alarmed that their privileged place on the campus might be usurped: "There were a few people in science who thought, well, here we go, we're going to end up with the tail wagging the dog sort of situation." Dissenters included some powerful men at the university, including Harry Duckworth and Howard Petch.

In June 1966, the matter of street diversion and the future of the proposed new complex came to a final head at city council. Copps called the decision the most difficult one council had had to face in years. While the city's technical experts were against the diversion because of potential traffic problems, Copps said the difference between a first-rate and a second-rate medical centre was more important. (The diversion required the immediate acquisition of 26 Westdale homes. The remaining homes in the blocks between Dalewood Avenue and Forsyth Avenue remained untouched.) To the immense relief of Harry Thode, the McMaster plan carried the day by a 12-8 vote. The war, at least this battle, was over. Thode had stuck to his guns and won the big one. But the controversies did not end with the selection of the site and the rerouting of streets.

McMaster had retained a highly respected firm of architects, one that had designed several hospitals across Canada, and was working on the largest medical science building in Canada, at the University of Toronto. From the point of view of reputation, this firm seemed a logical choice for the Health Sciences Centre at McMaster, but its vision failed to mesh with Thode's more ambitious and iconoclastic plans. By now, Thode, Evans, and others of the founders were in agreement that McMaster should put together a genuine health sciences centre, one in which not only a dramatically untraditional medical school would be established, but also, closely related, there would be programs for other types of health professionals, like nurses, physiotherapists, and occupational therapists, who would work closely in teams with other health professionals, including physicians.

John Evans, who had come to McMaster because it offered a better opportunity to innovate than did the University of Toronto, began to see the same sort of resistance to new ideas in the way the architects wanted to design the McMaster centre. He and his colleagues, with Thode's backing, had "worked very hard on the concept of what the medical school would be all about and the relationships that were going to be important; and so we believed that the relationships between people who were delivering the care and the scientists who were working in research and (medical) education should not be separated into classrooms in a didactic way and clinics in a clinical way. Therefore we could not have buildings that were divided into teaching sections, research sections and so on. We wanted to have the traffic of life in that building much more integrated."

Thode eventually decided that the many difficulties and differences between Evans and the architects had to be resolved by the university's board of governors. Any thought of changing the architects had to be approved by the board's building committee. Thode spent many hours with Evans and his colleagues: "They convinced me that we were never going to have the kind of medical school that John wanted and that we should have," said Thode, "if we went along with these Toronto architects. In other words, there were no new ideas going into it. It was just building the same thing that had been built everywhere else." That just was not good enough for Harry Thode.

By the time this debate reached its critical phase, it was the middle of 1967, and $250,000 had already been invested by the architects in their preliminary plans. To change course would throw off the scheduled completion of the centre, incur substantially more expenses, engender more unwelcome controversy, and diminish the reputation of one of Canada's leading architectural firms. The board of governors appeared bent on staying the course with existing plans. To convince them otherwise, Thode decided to seek outside help. He called in a New York architectural firm, one of the best teams of consultants in North America. They looked over the plans and came up with criticisms similar to those of John Evans. Their presentation to the board of governors changed enough minds and a decision was made to release the Toronto firm.

That Thode went along with such a drastic decision still amazes Evans. "Again I marvel at the naïveté in the board of governors and the president in not just telling us to stick with the existing architects. They were respected architects and they were doing the largest medical science building, one at the University of Toronto, and I do not think any other president would have tolerated this or understood it. They would just have seen it as a kind of factiousness of a bunch of young doctors who didn't know anything about it." Now McMaster had to start over. The decision, recalled Mike Hedden, "left a hell of a mess on our hands. It was touch and go. We had to come to terms with the architects and stave off losses."

On the advice of the New York consultants, McMaster hired Eberhard Zeidler, a Bauhaus-trained, German-born architect who had immigrated to Canada in 1951. Zeidler favoured strong technological themes in his design, and to the eventual distress of many, Evans and Thode did not pay much heed to what the exterior of the building would look like. Whether the outside looked like an oil refinery, as Duckworth would label it, or a combined factory (on its outside) and international hotel (inside) did not concern them. They were focused on the interior's potential to fulfil their vision of a functionally integrated clinical/research environment.

With Zeidler in place by the end of 1967, the next challenge was to recruit faculty and design a curriculum. When a new, unorthodox, and untried curriculum outline that emphasized more than academic performance in the sciences was submitted to the senate for approval, critics, especially from among the faculty of science's more traditional members, lined up to take a crack at it. The same resistance was heard when it came to approving appointments to the faculty. The senate was accustomed to seeing curricula vitae with the appointee's education crowned by a Ph.D., a record of research papers, and an appropriate number of teaching years consistent with the academic level of the appointment. But some of Evans's proposed appointments had no academic experience at all, and yet were being considered for assistant and associate professorships. These appointments would never have gone through if Thode had not strongly backed the experimental direction of the faculty of health sciences, says Evans.

For Evans, by far the most difficult job was recruiting staff. While Thode was willing to take big risks, he also urged patience. He warned Evans against "all the other problems you are going to create if you don't get the right decision with the best person—you're going to pay for it. He had been through all those things and, therefore, was an excellent mentor and backstop." There were, however, only a few academic physicians available to McMaster living in Canada. Shortly after construction of the health sciences centre was underway, Evans had contacted Dr. Moran Campbell at the Royal Postgraduate Medical School (Hammersmith) in the U.K., offering him the post of chairman of medicine. Moran was excited by the opening: "The idea of starting a new job in a new medical school, in a new country, rather than trying to reform an old medical school in an old country, had a certain attraction," Moran said in later years. He accepted the position and began to recruit promising faculty members.

One of the men who caught his eye was a young chap, Dr. E.S. (Steve) Garnett, who had been at Hammersmith since 1955. He had set up a small medical cyclotron, to provide radioactive fluorine-18 to serve as a marker for measuring blood flow in the brain, and Campbell saw his work fitting in well with the faculty's objectives, especially since McMaster had its own research reactor.

Garnett came to McMaster in 1969 and, with funding from Dofasco, established the first nuclear medicine department of any medical school in Canada. He also eventually set up McMaster's positron emission tomography (PET) scanner. In simple terms, it used positrons from radioactive fluorine-18 to scan sections of the brain and reveal the rate of blood flow in each area. In 1983, Garnett published a remarkable paper in *Nature*, showing how far he and his group had come in their research in the development of positron emission tomography. Garnett, colleagues said, realized the unique possibility of the PET scanner ten years before anyone else. Sadly, Garnett's exceptionally promising career was cut short by a fatal fall from a horse in September 1994.

Throughout all the trials of getting the Health Sciences Centre up and running, Evans never saw Thode lose control, nor did he appear, at least on the outside, to be suffering under the strain: "But I don't think there's any question that these were a new order of magnitude of problems to anything he'd experienced before in the development of the university," says Evans, "and so I think it was probably a tremendous worry. The severity of the problems that emerged was unanticipated."

Humble to a fault, Evans would suggest in later years that he was in large part to blame for a lot of the controversy over the health sciences centre. He still regrets the impression created that the university was a steamroller pushing everybody aside to realize its ambitions. The opposite was more the case, he says, because so many of the primary care services that were being developed within and related to the centre were intended to serve the community. The controversy, he believes, was useful for learning about Hamilton, but he thinks it was very costly in terms of the way he handled it. He says that he was not experienced or very effective in dealing with these problems and that someone else probably would have done a much better job in trying to maintain the support of the community and avoiding the type of confrontation that existed. Most who saw Evans in action, however, including Thode, would disagree. Evans was extraordinarily patient, explanatory, and gracious in dealings with a wide range of views and opinions, some of these openly hostile or wilfully uncomprehending.

Whatever mistakes Harry Thode made in getting the McMaster Health Sciences Centre built, the strength of his commitment to his objective never wavered, according to Evans. He recalls that the only point on which the two men differed concerned the involvement of other hospitals in the community. Evans wanted to include them all from the outset, but Thode, he sensed, saw the university hospital more as a research centre than a clinical hospital, and wanted to preserve some separation from other institutions in the community. Evans had a fuller vision of the clinical and social roles of the faculty and hospital than Thode did.

Thode won some important battles in the course of his struggle to bring health sciences to McMaster, but he was never out for his own glory. He fought hard but his goals were to challenge himself and others and make a contribution, not to defeat opponents or enhance his own stature. That is what John Evans learned most from Harry Thode. He saw the president of McMaster "in the swamps with the alligators," as he puts it, taking hits from the politicians and the public, and from his colleagues. But Thode always kept his vision, his objective, above the fray, and in the end, though with great difficulty and great pain and many imperfections, he was able to achieve it.

*Harry Thode with Carman McMullen (1985)*

*The McMaster University Health Sciences Centre*

# Chapter Twelve

# The President 1961-1972, Tensions in the Senior Administration

The controversy over the Health Sciences Centre plunged Thode into the worst years of his life. Inevitable power struggles in the leadership of the university added to his worries. The principal source of friction for Thode was Howard Petch. Petch was recognized as a leading light and possible successor to the presidency. Thode was uncomfortable with Petch's apparent hunger for power. "The relationship between the two was a good one for quite a while," recalls Arthur Bourns who became President in 1972. "But Petch was being more and more aggressive, and Harry saw him as a threat. I think that was part of the competitiveness of Thode. . . . Harry was able to delegate and was superb in that respect, but he wanted ultimate control. Petch was ambitious, and he not only wanted to control, he wanted to be seen to control. And that is something that Harry did not tolerate."

Petch allowed himself to become a sounding board for a few malcontents at the university, including those in the arts disciplines who had never liked the bias towards the sciences, which doubtless existed under Thode. Simmering differences grew through the mid-1960s. At this time, the rapidly expanding university prepared to overhaul its academic and administrative structure. A report prepared by Dr. J.S. (Jack) Kirkaldy, chairman of the department of metallurgy, recommended dissolution of the 19-year-old college system, in which Hamilton College was for sciences and University College was for the arts, and its replacement by three divisions: Science and Engineering, Arts, and Health Sciences. The 11-person committee, which headed by Kirkaldy and included Petch, reported that, under the current set-up, poor communications, duplication of effort, and conflict of authority constituted "a crisis" at the university. Thode, seeing the planned redistribution of power, was not keen on the proposed new structure, but it was approved by the university's governors without serious opposition from the president.

Appointments were made to head the new divisions. E. Togo Salmon became vice-president of arts. Salmon had considerable international stature and brilliance as a historian of ancient Rome, but, like other administrators, he had his weaknesses. He was sometimes brusque and cocksure, and lacking in diplomacy. He saw what needed to be done but pursued his agenda without exercising the patience necessary to build support. Arthur Bourns, single-minded in his commitment to scientific research and its funding, was made vice-president of science and engineering. John Evans, young, able, and relatively inexperienced, became vice-president of health sciences. The appointments took effect on July 1, 1967. Noticeably absent from the list was the name that many had expected to see, that of Howard Petch. Petch's exclusion from the new structure's top executive ranks signalled the end of his career at McMaster.

Thode had come to the conclusion that he could not work with Petch. He told Petch that it was not in his own best interests or the best interests of the university for him to become the science and engineering vice-president, leaving Petch with no choice but to quit. He moved on to the University of Waterloo as vice-president, and later became president of the University of Victoria, where he was able to fulfill much of the promise people had accurately seen in him.

When questioned in later years about the differences with Thode, Petch discounted the notion of a conflict between the two because of each man's ambition as the principal reason for his leaving McMaster. His explanation was that a difference of opinion with Thode over the future of Ontario's universities was at the heart of the matter. New universities were being established to accommodate ballooning enrolment in post-secondary education by the baby boom generation. Thode thought the newcomer institutions should concentrate on undergraduate programs while leaving graduate studies and research to established universities like his own. At one time, however, Thode had fought tooth and nail against the graduate studies and research establishment at the University of Toronto when its leadership sought to corner the market against upstarts like McMaster. But now he felt that graduate resources would be spread too thin if every university established doctoral programs. There would not be a sufficient number of top students to occupy all places available. Given McMaster's own history of standing up for the smaller schools, Petch could not abide such a contradiction: "I felt my philosophy was consistent with what we'd always tried to do at McMaster and that here was a change in our philosophy I couldn't accept."

Thode did favour an elitist approach to the growth of universities in Canada. He wanted a nurturing of the best, a "concentration of graduate teaching and research at the highest levels in a few universities across the country." If such programs were too widely available, he warned in a speech at the University of Toronto in 1965, "then we cannot expect to have a single university competitive with the graduate schools in the United States and Britain." He buttressed his argument by stating that, of the 2,400 universities and colleges in the United States, fewer than one hundred had first-rate graduate schools and that only a fraction of those received more than 80 per cent of Washington's support for university research. Research funds were awarded on the basis of merit and merit alone. "In my view there is no other area of human activity where the merit principle is more important than in research and other creative endeavours. . . . Any other basis will only encourage mediocrity."

He continued to reject the notion of state laboratories and institutes of the type favoured in the Soviet Union because they would draw talent away from the top universities: "The segregation of research in certain areas of science away from the universities can only lead to the fragmentation of science and of knowledge generally. . . . Only the universities can produce the first-class scientists," he asserted.

While philosophical differences probably were instrumental in the rift between Petch and Thode, Arthur Bourns says that to call these the fundamental reason for the split is "plain nonsense." The real reason, he says, was that "Harry saw Petch as a threat." The conflict between the two men was unfortunate, because many at McMaster, including Thode loyalists like Bourns and John Evans, thought Petch would have made an outstanding successor to Harry Thode.

"Harry made some mistakes and so did Petch," recalls Sadie Thode of the dispute. She shares the view of others that, when Thode gave Petch authority, he tended to take it too far; his style differed from that of Thode, who preferred a more genial manner of management. Thode grew frustrated with taking the flack from colleagues offended by what they saw as Petch's overstepping. In the end, says Sadie, "I think he may have felt he promoted Petch a little too fast."

Petch's difference with Thode over the location of the Health Sciences Centre was another irritant in their relationship, notes Jack Kirkaldy. Kirkaldy was a close friend of Howard Petch. They had been graduate students together at the University of British Columbia. At McMaster they used to take their lunch breaks in the Royal Botanical Gardens, where they would sit on the lawns and eat their sandwiches while watching the goldfish swim in the ponds. They both mourned the loss of this part of the Gardens and worried that the health sciences centre would dwarf other priorities on the campus.

Relations between Thode and Harry Duckworth also had been strained. Two years earlier, Duckworth had left to go to the University of Manitoba as vice-president. Duckworth was another talented, ambitious man. There being room for only one president, he chose to leave. Martin Johns recalls that Duckworth wanted Thode's job. "Duckworth hadn't left here feeling completely happy with things, you know. I think it was the problem of who was to be the president. It was to be either Harry Duckworth or Harry Thode."

In his report on the restructuring of McMaster, John Kirkaldy weighed the positive and negative aspects of Thode's stewardship: "Our standing in the provincial, national, and international scene and the calibre of students entering McMaster have continued to advance dramatically during a period when our public relations with the citizens of Hamilton appear to have deteriorated," the report stated. It drew attention to a breakdown of internal campus communications which, it said, contributed to the confusion during the controversy over the Health Sciences Centre. "Communications within and without the university were ineffective and many misunderstandings arose. . . . There is a deep feeling that we should reform ourselves in such a way that difficulties of this sort will be avoided in the future." Kirkaldy warned that "most members of the university community, students, faculty and Board members, live inside bubbles, and these will not easily be punctured."

Without reform, Kirkaldy said, the university risked more interference from government, owing to the increasing public subsidies that were going into university education. "It is this spectre which makes it imperative that the various [university] constituencies . . . resolve their differences."

The *Hamilton Spectator* said that, while McMaster was seemingly as organized as any university in the province, it still had to get its house in order: "If it is not to be swamped by Big Brother in Queen's Park, the university of the future is going to have to function as an administrative unit with its various disciplines and endeavours sufficiently integrated so that the left hand knows what the right hand is doing." It is perhaps ironic that Thode was criticized for internal divisions within the campus, when he was always a champion of integration and efforts to encourage interdisciplinary activity. Integration of research and educational activities, however, is not the same thing as effective administrative procedures. As rapid growth continued at McMaster, the earlier relatively autocratic style of administration was giving way to a far greater pluralism of intellectual ambitions and responsibilities.

Reflecting on his report from the perspective of the 1990s, the blunt-spoken Kirkaldy is pleased that its essence was accepted by subsequent and current administrators, but he speaks of the frustrations of not being able to go as far as he wished: "We were obstructed in all directions," he recalls. "I wanted to get into the financial end, the books. They [the administration] wouldn't let me." He sensed that there was too much bureaucracy, that the administration of the university could have been streamlined to accomplish major savings. He complained to Thode, but got the impression that the president wanted to keep the books closed.

During the sixties, universities were getting so much money from government that they did not know what to do with it all, Kirkaldy recalls. Administrators would find ways of using grants for other purposes than those for which they were intended: "I saw this going on in Harry's administration and got very upset," says the former metallurgy chairman. For example, Kirkaldy says that he found $2 million in government monies that were supposed to go into operations but instead went to purchase a computer for research. He kept silent about these incidents in light of Thode's opposition to opening the university's books to scrutiny. (Arthur Bourns disagrees with Kirkaldy's interpretation, pointing out that the computer was used for teaching as well as research. Any suggestions that government monies were misspent are inaccurate, Bourns states.)

Kirkaldy remembers that, when confronted with complaints, Thode deftly moved the discussion off-topic so that he would not have to answer tough questions. In the middle of a discussion about improvements in the administration, for example, Thode would start talking about sulphur isotopes, a topic on which he could ruminate endlessly. Kirkaldy, as tough-spoken as he was, did not like to challenge his boss too directly: "I never raised my voice to him. I was afraid to do that." He now regrets not confronting Thode on the subject of the money-losing nuclear reactor. As early as the mid-sixties, it was not being put to good use: "It was already starting the bleeding." Kirkaldy also wanted to make the executive selection process at the university more democratic. He unsuccessfully challenged the right of the board of governors to appoint the president, wanting this major responsibility to be open to more voices.

Kirkaldy appreciated the fact that Thode did not mind having "prickly pears" around him. Thode was, Kirkaldy believes, neither a top administrator nor a good teacher, but his vision and his determination to carry out this vision outweighed such shortcomings. The goal of making McMaster the MIT of Canada appealed to Kirkaldy, and he supported Thode all the way in that aim. Though McMaster did not quite make it, that it got as close as it did is remarkable, given its humble beginnings. The achievement is a tribute to Thode's special talents, says Kirkaldy.

Peter George, who was to become president of McMaster in 1995, came to the university as a junior lecturer in economics in 1964. He was amazed to be given an audience with Thode, who welcomed him warmly to the campus.

As George witnessed the conflict and upheaval the university was experiencing on so many fronts, he was impressed by the calm at the centre. "My perception throughout it all was that it was sort of guided by an unseen hand; you know, it's like a classical economic description of the market economy. I never had the sense that we were being pushed or prodded, so maybe it goes back to [Thode's] power of persuasion and the model of a profound belief in the integration of education and scholarship and research."

The sixties and early seventies were the fractious years of hippies and drugs and counter-culture and campus protest, but at McMaster there was a respected father figure who kept the lid on. Thode had a reputation among the students as a scientist of renown. He was low-key in his bearing and pronouncements. To young students who paid little attention to the administration's infighting, he stood with almost papal detachment above the clamour, a dignified figure of learning.

In the late sixties, Dermot Nolan was active in the student government and was chairman of the students representative assembly. He had dealings with Thode over the question of students having more say in the running of the university. They wanted, for example, representation on the university senate, and they got it. "It was almost impossible to get angry at Thode, no matter what the issue," recalls the former history student. "There were some issues on which I would go in to see him, and I had a full head of steam worked up and I was going to give him hell. Then I'd get in his office and within a minute my fires would be out." Nolan explains that it was more Thode's manner and reputation than anything the president did or said that defused conflict: "You had the feeling that he was wise and understanding and so you didn't want to challenge him. You thought it would be almost sacrilegious to raise your voice in his presence."

Editors of the student paper, *The Silhouette*, echo these impressions. Unlike many campus papers of the era, *The Silhouette* was not a left-wing radical sheet that levelled broadsides at anybody in a suit. Still, it was at times heavily critical of the way the university was run. The attacks, however, were rarely aimed at Thode: "I recall there were a lot of other turkeys around there when I was editor of the paper in 1968-69," says Albert Cipryk, "and we had fun taking them down a peg. But Thode had this terrific reputation. You had the feeling he was above it all." "We [the students] weren't really sure what kind of reputation McMaster had when we went there. We used to sort of mock the place, as if it was sub-standard. But one thing we did know was that we had a president who was right up there with the best. In a way, he made us proud to be there." Thode once took Cipryk on a tour of the nuclear reactor. The president spent a couple of hours trying to explain to the editor how it worked. Cipryk was an arts student and, like some arts students, did not know an atom from an apple, but Thode explained in such basic lay terms that Cipryk was able to write a full-page feature story on the reactor.

Physicist Mel Preston became dean of graduate studies in 1965 and remained in the position until 1971. This was a period of major growth in graduate studies, including at McMaster. At one point, Preston had intended to leave the university to go to Winnipeg with Duckworth, but a rumour to that effect prompted Thode to offer him the graduate deanship. Preston rapidly became a formidable academic administrator, who made himself perhaps the best informed person on campus about the academic strengths, weaknesses, and activities in the departments across the six faculties. Deeply and rigorously involved in the making of faculty appointments and in considerations for tenure and promotion, Preston exerted major influence not only on graduate developments, but also on the emerging research and scholarly strengths of McMaster as a whole. As dean, he advised Thode of the fact that the arts areas of McMaster were ready for a higher level of development. With Thode's assent, he was the major architect of a wide range of new programs.

Alvin Lee, a future president of the university, came to McMaster to the English department in 1960, at the close of the Gilmour era, having turned down Yale and some of the most prestigious universities in the U.S., as well as a flattering number in Canada. As he wryly remarks, "Anyone finishing a Ph.D. in 1960 who had any vital signs was highly marketable. In a major subject like English, with a specialization in Old English, you could almost write your own ticket." His introduction to administration and to university-wide responsibilities was as assistant dean of graduate studies, beginning in 1968 and working closely with Preston. He had the sense well before that, however, one day in 1962, that he had made the right choice of university, when he and a colleague went to see the dean of graduate studies, Harry Duckworth. They discussed the message that was coming down from the administration to several of the arts departments, that it was time to develop doctoral programs. They talked about the willingness of newly appointed ambitious young scholars in these departments to begin such work. But they were concerned that there was no realistic sense in the senior administration of the financial implications. The first step toward the goal was a proper humanities and social sciences research library. Asked by Duckworth how much that would cost, Lee said a million dollars in library acquisitions each year for a decade, to make a significant start. Before many months passed, the request was acted on, and Lee knew that Thode was behind the approval.

Lee recalls Thode as saying, in a conversation about an administrative appointment in arts, that he wanted McMaster to be not only another MIT but a combination of Princeton and MIT: "At that time in his career, he wanted us to be topnotch in both arts and sciences. Sometimes, in other contexts, he said Stanford instead of MIT. What he meant was research depth and educational excellence across the university. I think that that conception got well established in the minds of a lot of people here, especially the younger faculty members, during Thode's presidency in the 1960s."

Lee was impressed that, at McMaster, they did not take many academic quality shortcuts, as he knew some other universities did, in matters like awarding tenure if a professor had not earned it. When mistakes in faculty appointments were made, a fair number of these were corrected before it was too late. "McMaster set the standards high in research. They put in place an infrastructure to help faculty members win research grants in external competitions. They put up the buildings and created the laboratories. They paid competitive salaries. In due course, they began building impressive library facilities and collections." During Thode's presidency, McMaster was an excellent place for able scholars in any discipline represented in the university. McMaster was developing as a fairly inclusive academic entity, even though, even at the time, this was not Thode's main personal ambition for McMaster. Money was relatively plentiful, and he respected excellence when he saw it emerge. As the 1960s came to a close, McMaster, the house that Harry built, was taking its rightful place in the first ranks of Canadian universities. It was strong and prestigious in science, and developing to a high level in engineering, health sciences, humanities, and social sciences, with pockets of real strength beginning to emerge in commerce.

*A. Lee (1983) – Alvin A. Lee, a future president of the university, came to McMaster to the English department in 1960*

*McMaster University Campus (c. 1970)*

115

# Chapter Thirteen

## The Russell Archives, New Doctoral Programs and Professional Schools, Gender Equity, Thode's Research on Moon Rocks

In the fall of 1967, William Ready, the chief librarian at McMaster, was travelling by train from London's Paddington Station to Cardiff, Wales. He picked up a copy of the *Sunday Times* and noticed an article about the disposition of the papers of British philosopher and mathematician Bertrand Russell. The story revealed that the papers, which spanned 90 years of Russell's life and included thousands of letters, films, tapes, and manuscripts, were coming up for sale. The *Times* estimated the price at $2 million. William Ready returned to Canada a few days later intent on the far-fetched idea of procuring the Russell archive for a Canadian university, McMaster being his natural first choice. Landing the papers would put the successful library in the forefront of international scholarship, Ready calculated.

Ready took his idea to Thode, who immediately gave his approval to an aggressive effort by McMaster to get the papers. Ready won support from university librarians in Ontario to approach the Canada Council for a major grant toward the acquisition. The lone dissenting voice came from the University of Toronto, which coveted the archive for itself. The Council came back with the good word that it was prepared to assist McMaster in the amount of $150,000.

Ready wrote Lord Russell describing McMaster in the most flattering terms. He mentioned Thode's being a Fellow of the Royal Society, as was Russell, and praised the president's distinguished record in science. Emphasizing the British connection, he described vice-president of arts Togo Salmon's background as a Cambridge scholar. Russell responded with cordial letters and the agent for the sale of his papers was dispatched to McMaster. The agent was greatly impressed by what he saw and further encouraged by Ready's promise that there would be no problem in raising the funds for making the purchase.

Ready had obtained $25,000 from financier and McMaster alumnus Cyrus Eaton, but progress in securing other support was slow. With the deadline for submitting a formal bid at hand, he was still $200,000 short of the amount needed. Thode, who was well versed in the art of fundraising, told Ready of the generous support which the Atkinson Foundation had helped provide for a nursing school at McMaster in the late forties. Ready approached the Atkinson representative, who readily agreed to contribute the necessary funding.

Ready set out again for England hoping against hope to succeed against competition from many of the world's leading university institutions. Happily for Ready, the idea of little-known McMaster University in Hamilton, Canada, had captured Lord Russell's fancy, and Ready's bid was approved. For Ready, it was the coup of a lifetime. McMaster the underdog, at what some thought of as the science school, had landed one of the literary treasures of the century. The *Toronto Star* waxed enthusiastic: "When you think of Hamilton, do you think of an ugly harbour, some grimy mills and the Tiger-Cat football team? Well, now you'll have to think again because yesterday, while few people noticed it, quietly and anonymously, culture came to the Steel City! . . . From now on, when you think of Hamilton, you'll have to think of it also as Canada's cradle of philosophy, containing the archives and personal papers of the world's oldest and most famous peacenik. Last month McMaster University in Hamilton pulled off the biggest literary and academic coup in Canada's history by buying the papers, despite serious competition from big, rich American and British institutions."

With the transaction successfully concluded, Lord Russell asked Ready to celebrate with him over tea at Russell's home. Ready awoke the next morning to hear that his mother had died during the night at her home in Wales. He asked the university's lawyer, Frank Weatherston, to take his place at Lord Russell's tea table. Somehow news of the change did not come through clearly to Lord Russell, who was almost 96. The philosopher began putting questions to Weatherston as if he were William Ready, all kinds of questions about archival details to which Weatherston had to play dumb. Later, Lord Russell commented how curious it was that Ready in the flesh did not seem the same man with whom he had conducted correspondence in the past.

As a delighted Thode told colleagues, the Russell Papers were for the arts at McMaster what the reactor was for the sciences. McMaster was the first university in the Commonwealth to get a nuclear reactor, it had built one of the leading health sciences institutions in the country, and now, as Ready put it, it "became known throughout the length and breadth of the world of English."

Some British scholars were appalled at Russell's decision: "There was a great deal of comment when it was finally realized the extent and significance of the papers that had left England," recalls Ready, "and the rows that built in the newspapers and elsewhere increased in volume until they reached such a pitch that I received a call from the *London Observer* questioning me as to what action the Canadian government would take if Britain demanded the return of the papers."

Thode also had to stand up to opposition from certain members of the board of governors who objected to the expense of the acquisition, certainly a modest one in comparison with sums being invested at the time in science, engineering, and health sciences. He was heavily criticized by some of the university fathers, not just for the money, but for wanting Russell's works in the first place. The philosopher's liberal views on sexual matters and his antinuclear pacifism and condemnation of the Vietnam war had aroused the ire of conservatives among McMaster's faculty, but Thode was unmoved by their protests.

In December 1967, McMaster lost one of its greatest builders, E. Carey Fox, who had begun his association with the university as a student in 1902. Fox spent more than fifty years as a member of both the senate and the board of governors, where his emphasis was always on high standards in faculty scholarship and curriculum development. Harry Thode had profited greatly from Fox's wisdom and support. Fox had stood behind Thode on many contentious issues.

In the summer of 1969, Thode provided a status report on McMaster and its future to the board of governors. He spoke of the establishment of the professional schools: engineering in 1958, commerce and business from 1954 through 1964, health sciences in 1966, and social work in 1968. For future expansion he envisaged a law school and a faculty of education coming to McMaster in the early 1970s. The law school never materialized, despite Thode's assertion that "it is our intention to establish this faculty to fill a gap in our program and to fill an urgent need in the Hamilton area." The flood of law graduates that was issuing from the University of Toronto, Western, Queen's, and Ottawa left many observers thinking that McMaster should not establish a law school, and time proved them right. Plans to establish a faculty of education proceeded slowly. Initially, it was proposed that teacher education should be the responsibility of a new department in the faculty of humanities, rather than a faculty of education. This was unacceptable to the Ministry of Education. By the time the university finally put forward an acceptable proposal, it was too late. A surplus of new teacher graduates had developed, and Brock University, which had established a large education faculty some years earlier, was more than able to meet the need. McMaster was told to abandon its plans. This could hardly be considered a serious disappointment: the university had a large challenge at the time in the mounting of its faculty of health sciences.

Thode outlined with pride the development of McMaster's graduate programs. It was he who, in 1949, provided the impetus to start Ph.D. programs in the physical sciences. They were followed shortly with doctoral studies in mathematics, biology, and engineering. Now, the president noted, McMaster had 17 doctoral programs in pure and applied sciences. In the arts, development was more recent, but doctoral programs had been established in English, geography, history, religious studies, Roman studies, and economics. Political science and sociology would soon be added to the list. Although not mentioned by Thode but on the drawing board, so would anthropology and philosophy (the latter jointly with the University of Guelph). "Another measure of the size and excellence of our graduate research program is the annual grants-in-aid of graduate research work which professors are able to attract from government, industry and other agencies." This total was well over $5 million annually, reported Thode.

Enrolment when Thode arrived at the university in 1939 was 500 a year. In the 1950s it had jumped to 1,000 full-time students and now McMaster was accepting roughly 6,000 full-time students annually. Full-time graduate students comprised 17 percent of McMaster's enrolment.

As the university continued to expand, a new challenge faced Thode. Like other universities (except those exclusively for women), McMaster's faculty reflected a significant imbalance in the proportion of men to women among the faculty. Thode was pushed into the vanguard in confronting this issue when sociologist Lynn McDonald presented a brief to the senate, chaired by Thode, which purported to detail systemic bias against female academics at McMaster. McDonald charged that the attitude toward progress for women, that is, the attitude among the administrators, was that, if women were not in senior positions, it was because they did not deserve to be. She was relieved to find Thode liberal in his views: "Harry could have said that, but he didn't. He did take it seriously, and he did agree to a process, a rather unsatisfactory process, but nonetheless it was a process." It was a very strained meeting, she recalls, with a good deal of animosity in the air, but Thode's calm approach helped relax the tension. Knowing him to be a traditionalist with a background in a scientific discipline practised by very few women, she was pleasantly surprised to find Thode so open to her proposals. "No doubt it [the brief] broke new ground," asserts McDonald, "absolutely broke new ground. And I guess one could speculate that if Harry had opposed it, what would have happened then? Would other universities have made the breakthrough?" The committee named to develop policies to ensure gender equity for McMaster faculty had three members, Arthur Bourns, Alvin Lee, and Doris Jensen, a female biologist. Within the academic year their recommendations were readily adopted by the senate as university policy.

For Thode, breakthroughs in campus politics no doubt paled beside the earthshaking event that occurred on July 20, 1969, when man first set foot on the moon. Thode had already submitted a request for samples of any moon rocks that were collected from a successful lunar-landing mission. Thode had learned that the National Aeronautics and Space Administration had set up a research committee to offer advice on how to distribute the lunar samplings. As an esteemed scientist and expert in sulphur isotopes, Thode was reasonably confident he would be chosen to receive moon rocks for study, but months went by and he heard nothing. After the moon landing there was still no news; it was almost a year after the historic event that he found out why.

In 1970, he took a six-month sabbatical to do research at one of his favourite universities, the California Institute of Technology. The timing was fortunate because it allowed him to miss a sit-in of the president's office at McMaster. Arthur Bourns, Thode's interim replacement, one spring day, found his quarters occupied by students protesting food prices and services on campus. It is intriguing to speculate on how Thode would have reacted to this protest or whether the students would have dared occupy the office had Thode been present. He was impressed by the way Bourns handled the matter. Rather than risk intensifying the controversy by being confrontational, Bourns let the students remain in his office a few days, until they were satisfied the university would address their demands.

Thode loved his year away from the pressures of running McMaster. He could concentrate fully on research without the myriad distractions of administrative duties. While lunching at Cal Tech with Gerry Wasserburg, a distinguished physicist who was on the advisory committee for assigning lunar samples, Thode was told he had applied too late, that he should have applied two years earlier. Those who knew him, and his lack of passion for administrative detail, would not be astonished to learn that he had missed the application deadline. He was disappointed nonetheless. Wasserburg did promise that Thode would receive samples from the next Apollo mission.

Thode's interest in the moon samplings went back many years: Harold Urey, his early mentor, had done studies on the moon's surface two decades earlier. Urey had appeared at the opening of the nuclear building at McMaster in 1950 and speculated on the origin and chemical formation of the lunar material. Said Thode: "Long before any samples were returned from the moon or even before the first moon landing occurred, he had, of course, contemplated the scientific issues that he expected to be resolved by the space program."Alex Roncari, who worked as an ultrasound specialist in the nuclear building, was on the scene when the moon samples arrived at McMaster: "That was the greatest excitement we had in this university and in this building for many many years. That was the pièce de résistance. We were all waiting to see, to touch, to approach that specimen from the moon at McMaster in the hot lab and seeing Dr. Thode handling it and analyzing it. That was the climax of my career."

Because of his knowledge of sulphur and its isotopes, Thode had a particular fascination for the moon rocks. Sulphur occurs in different forms depending on how it is produced, whether naturally or through a biological process. It was possible for Thode to look at sulphur isotopes as a kind of fingerprint to shed light on the origin of the moon and the subsequent geological processes that occurred on its surface. He publicly displayed the moon rocks at McMaster, which attracted thousands of visitors and, like the Russell archive, substantially added to both the university's local and international reputations.

Working with his brilliant young colleague Charles E. Rees, Thode published his first paper on sulphur concentration and isotope ratios in Apollo 12 samples soon after they arrived in his lab. He and Rees published 11 more papers throughout the 1970s, following his retirement in June 1972 as McMaster president. Their fundamental research about the origins of the moon has stood the test of time, notes their McMaster colleague Henry Schwarz, who also took part in the research: "I think their observations about how these samples obtained their curious varieties of isotopic composition are still the established wisdom on the subject," says Schwarz.

Thode had been in Moscow during the time when the Soviets revealed pictures of the moon taken from their unmanned lunar probes. He drolly recalled being at a luncheon with the distinguished Russian scientists Peter Kapitza and Nikolay Nikolayevich Semenov when Kapitza described the image of the moon as "just like Semenov's head over there, as bald as a billiard ball."

The research on the moon rocks, especially the initial quantities, was very difficult, because the traces of sulphur in them were very small. Thode's passion for the undertaking showed that his love of research was still intense. Alvin Lee, who, in the spring of 1971, was stepping down as assistant dean of graduate studies and was arranging for his family of seven to spend a year in Oxford, recalls Thode arriving one Saturday morning in his driveway to try and convince him that he should become dean of graduate studies (Mel Preston was moving to a province-wide graduate planning position for the Council of Ontario Universities): "I remember very clearly how, after a little discussion of the appointment proposal, we stood out on the driveway in the sunshine, and he talked for about an hour about his work on moon rocks." Thode knew that Lee's interests, as a professor of literature, were far afield from moon rocks, but he was so caught up in his research that he went on and on, rapt in the subject.

"It was illuminating," recalls Lee, "because Harry did it in such a way that I at least partly understood what he was saying. . . . I had a strong sense of, here's a guy who is still luminous with his science after spending years building an institution and monitoring it. I remember thinking, as he drove away, if he can still be a scientist and take all that administrative work as well, maybe I can take the risk, because I would still be able to be primarily a scholar." Lee dropped plans for his year in Oxford and took Thode up on his offer, carving out a distinguished career both in administration and in literary scholarship.

While the moon rocks preoccupied Thode, he took great interest in even more esoteric research, things like sulphur isotope ratios in the mud in the bottom of the Black Sea. He had begun his career as a physical chemist, moved to physics, and subsequently shifted to geology and geochemistry. Sulphur, the essential ingredient of most ore deposits, is what most fascinated him. It is the binding element that holds together lead, zinc, copper, and, to some extent, silver and gold. Learning about sulphur and its isotopes was to learn about the origin and nature of ore deposits. For example, Thode studied the sulphur isotope behaviour of the enormous gold deposit found at Hemlo in northwestern Ontario. Sulphur is also a constituent of acid rain and a contributor to a lot of environmental problems. One way to study the behaviour of sulphur in the environment and get at the source of acid rain is to follow the variations of the isotope ratios.

Along with Jan Monster, Thode also did work on the sulphur isotope composition of the salt that crystallizes out of seawater. "This study," said Schwarz, was "a tremendous revelation to scientists about how much variation there had been in the earth's environment over the last six hundred million years. I think that people sometimes forget the fact that he made these original insights into this field."

Thode's continuing explorations demonstrated his adherence to his guiding principle that research must be a critical priority for a university. To students who claimed that universities were increasingly emphasizing their research programs at the expense of teaching, Thode responded, "these kinds of arguments have been present as long as I can remember. There are always a few teachers who can be criticized for putting too little attention on teaching. But it's been my experience that the best teachers were always those who worked on the border of the unknown, the professors who brought their enthusiasm for their research into the classroom."

*Harry Thode with Ted Rees (1981)*

# Chapter Fourteen

# Thode Finishes His Presidency

By the fall of 1971, Thode had completed more than a decade as president and had fulfilled his main ambitions. McMaster was a leading sciences research institution; a cutting-edge health sciences centre had been established against heavy odds; and the faculties of engineering, humanities, and social sciences, through the 1960s, had expanded to include many doctoral programs, several of which shortly were to rank among the few best in Canada. At the same time, all the faculties were heavily engaged in teaching a greatly expanded population of undergraduates.

The administrative burden and the controversies had taken their toll on 61-year old Thode, who was willing to admit that he did not have the drive he once had. He had known other university presidents who had stayed too long in their jobs, and his family was trying gently to persuade him to step down. They had never thought he was ideally cut out for the job of the day-to-day running of an institution as large as McMaster had become. "I think," recalls son Pat, "that he was trying from the very beginning to get out of it, but didn't know how to say no to people. He didn't know the way out. His personality didn't allow him to escape."

Though Thode had appointed several able men to support him, he had been unable or unwilling to shed many of the most taxing responsibilities. Between 1961and 1972, while president, chairman of the senate, a member of the board of governors, and the university's public representative (local, provincial, national, and international), Thode published 17 scholarly scientific papers. He served on the board of governors of the Ontario Research Foundation and as its vice-chairman from 1970-1972. He was a member of the International Union of Pure and Applied Chemistry from 1963 to 1974. He was a member of the board of trustees of the Western New York Nuclear Research Center and a consultant for Brookhaven National Laboratories. Between 1966 and 1970, he served on the board of the National Museum of Science and Technology. He was a director and member of the executive committee of Atomic Energy of Canada Limited, a director of Stelco Inc., and vice-chairman of the Council of Presidents of the Universities of Ontario. Thode was proud of these achievements as an administrator and public representative of the university, but his first love was still research.

On November 12, 1971, he tendered his letter of resignation, which expressed his desire to return to teaching and research until he reached retirement: "By next spring I will have served on the McMaster faculty for a total of thirty-three years, twelve of those as principal of Hamilton College and vice-president, and the last eleven as president," Thode wrote. "I am convinced that it would now be in the best interest of the university to have the advantages of a change in leadership. It is for this reason that I am tendering my resignation . . . . I am honoured to have served as president of McMaster. Although there have been trials and tribulations, it has been a challenge and great fun. I know that McMaster will continue to develop and serve the community as an enlightened place of learning."

At a meeting of the board of governors on November 23, chairman Robert Taylor gave an overview of Thode's career, his words neatly summarizing, without resorting to the overstatement that such occasions usually summon, what Thode had meant to McMaster:

> As we reflect upon this development [Thode's retirement], we recall that Dr. Thode has been a member of McMaster University since 1939. He came to this campus as a young man filled with an intense interest in research—the kind of research that leads scholars to the frontiers of knowledge and beyond. Even then his reputation as a scientist was of such high order that he was asked to participate in a vital government research project in atomic energy. Not far from here, in Hamilton Hall, he established and carried out much of this exciting and challenging work. A further mark of tribute to Dr. Thode was the approval of the establishment during the fifties of McMaster's nuclear reactor, the first such facility to be located on a university campus in Canada.
> The postwar period brought a great surge of student interest in the sciences and as a result McMaster decided to set up Hamilton College for the development of such studies. It was natural that Dr. Thode should be chosen as first principal of the college in 1948. From that day to this he has devoted much of his energy to encouraging graduate work and research at the Ph.D. level and beyond. As one would expect, the first doctoral program was approved in his own field of chemistry followed closely by a similar program in physics. It is no accident that these two departments continue to be outstanding in activity and achievement.

> Dr. Thode was a prime mover in the creation of our engineering school during a period of extremely rapid growth of the university. He was a

tower of strength when it was decided that McMaster should become a nondenominational university in 1957. From that day until he took office as president in 1961, he was not only principal of Hamilton College but also vice-president of the university and the strong right hand of the late George P. Gilmour during those demanding times.

His appointment to the presidency in 1961 was widely hailed. As president, his humane and humble attitude has kept his door open at all times to any member of the faculty, staff or student body who wished to see him. He had always sought to achieve communication and mutual confidence in all his day-to-day relationships, and these had contributed greatly to the warm admiration that all members of this community felt for him.

The impetus that he gave to the development of graduate and research programs in science has been matched by the support he has provided to establish similar programs in the arts. Moreover, the deep interest he felt for medicine and his participation in medical research for many years found full expression when McMaster established the College of Health Sciences in 1965. His labours before and after that date have helped produce one of the most imaginative medical schools and health sciences centres on the North American continent.

As though all of this were not enough, he provided the energetic leadership necessary to reform the deliberative and administrative structure of the university and make it more responsive and effective in carrying out its important tasks. Time after time his voice has been raised in the cause of Canadian science, where he has been an effective champion of fundamental research.

Honours have deservedly come to him for his tremendous contributions to so many scientific, national and community projects. He is one of the few Canadians to have been made a Fellow of the Royal Society (London). He is a valued member of the executive committee of Atomic Energy of Canada Limited. Further distinctions are his fellowships in the Royal Society of Canada, Chemical Institute of Canada and other learned societies. In the centennial year of 1967, he was appointed as one of the first and select Companions of the Order of Canada. Eight universities have conferred on him their honorary degrees.

It is amazing that, despite these outstanding accomplishments, he has found the energy for his active research and the time he devotes to graduate students and post-doctorate fellows. This work has kept him in the forefront of his field as a productive scholar and scientist, respected by his colleagues around the world. It is fitting therefore that after his leave of absence he intends to return to McMaster and continue the work he loves best—teaching and research.

This board is grateful to him for his years of service and leadership to McMaster. We wish him good health and many happy and fulfilling years.

Thode still had a few months left before he formally stepped down. He continued to wield his influence. One intervention was in response to the report of the Senate Special Committee on Science Policy (Lamontagne Committee), which had recommended the revamping of the administration of science, taking power away from the National Research Council and dispersing it, as Thode interpreted the report, into a maze of foundations, boards, institutes, task forces, and committees. Thode issued a strong rebuke in the publication *Science Forum*, pointing out that "in recommending this drastic change in the structure of government science, involving complete dismemberment of the National Research Council, the committee has chosen to ignore the historical development of science in Canada." Spreading research and development oversight to several bodies "would set Canadian science back many years," he warned.

Thode had developed a close relationship with the National Research Council over the decades. The council had organized and directed Canadian research during the war years, provided major support for the creation of research installations such as the McMaster reactor, and provided grants to Canada's universities and industries and support for Canada's most promising young scientists. Thode felt he understood the N.R.C.'s accomplishments better than the senators on the Lamontagne Committee. He was committed to protecting its legacy.

His defence of the N.R.C. did not mean that he always agreed with its dealings. After the dispute over the committee report, he fought the council over a change in its awarding of grants. They had shifted one of his grant applications to the chemistry selection committee over to the earth sciences selection committee. "I am most distressed that this decision was made, apparently last summer, without my knowledge," he wrote. "I realize that my research program is interdisciplinary and involves physics, chemistry, and earth sciences; however I feel that the chemistry selection committee, which has considered my applications in the past, is the most appropriate single committee. I would, therefore, like to appeal the decision made last summer."

Closer to home, he was leaving clues, albeit understated, for the direction he wished McMaster to take after he stepped down. In a speech delivered on Graduates' Day, May 29, 1971, he made it clear that McMaster could not become a university that was trying to be all things to all people. It had to focus on its strengths: "No university can be tops in everything, not even Harvard. A university must decide on its priorities over the whole range of legitimate objectives. . . . We must establish ours. It's imperative that we do, otherwise we will be swept along toward mediocrity by the many external and internal pressures we face. With formula financing in Ontario, there is a tendency to force all the universities into a common mold." This principle of selective excellence rather than comprehensive mediocrity was already systematically in use at McMaster. Under the leadership of Mel Preston and Alvin Lee as dean and assistant dean, respectively, of graduate studies, specific areas within some disciplines were being chosen for development. Other areas or sub-disciplines were left to other graduate schools. History, for example, had a strong doctoral program, but it was in modern European history, not the whole chronological or geographic range of the subject. Civil engineering emphasized transportation and earthquake engineering. There was no doctoral program in classics but there was a strong one in the particular McMaster strength, Roman studies. No doctoral development was planned in computer science, this subject being recognized as a leading edge of the universities of Toronto and Waterloo. McMaster had relatively few of the disciplines found in "professional" faculties or schools, like architecture, dentistry, education, forestry, law, or optometry. It was soon to develop a strong management science program within the business faculty. Its school of nursing, now within health sciences, was making changes that would transform it into an international model. The school of social work was concentrating on one important area, social welfare policy.

On the Graduates' Day a year before he left the presidency, Thode also told the graduates that the university had to determine its optimum enrolment, which he put at about 12,000 students. Decades before the advent of the Internet, he predicted that advances in electronic communications and networks would mean that facilities like the university library need not grow at a rate once thought: "Our library is part of a much larger library system of the universities of Ontario, a transport system which travels from Windsor through London, Waterloo, Hamilton, Toronto, Kingston and to Ottawa every day, and picks up and drops off books and journals at each university." In fact, by 1971, the principle of interlibrary cooperation among the universities of Ontario—in the acquisition, cataloguing, and circulation of books, journals, and other materials—was vigorously in effect. The basis also was being laid for cooperation with library systems much more comprehensive than that of Ontario's universities.

One of Thode's main emphases throughout most of his career was toward interdisciplinary cooperation. In his 1971 report he made special mention of the Health Sciences Centre in this regard. Its concept, he noted, was "based on the view that delivery of health care is a team responsibility shared by many people with different types of training. While each health profession had a specific educational requirement, by training together in shared facilities, a unique opportunity existed for establishing effective inter-professional working relations."

Thode's having spent 32 years at McMaster had not dulled his thirst for change, in teaching, curriculum reform, and curriculum experimentation. A university senate committee on undergraduate education had been studying such matters for two years, and it delivered a report, the Vichert Report, with some 70 recommendations. Thode appeared to favour a controversial recommendation, firmly rejected by the majority of faculty, that advocated a heavily diminished supervision of undergraduate study. Thode wanted less emphasis on the lecture system with its large classes, and more informal study programs that would create closer relationships between faculty and students. There was significant faculty interest in this aspect of the report, but this was overwhelmed by the ways in which the proposed reduction of lectures seemed to point to the dismantling of honours degree programs, and to a probable drop in intellectual expectations and achievements.

The May 1972 formal opening of the Health Sciences Centre was a glorious day for Thode. To be sure, what some call the "brutalist" architecture of the massive grey building had few admirers. To some people it looked like a prison fortress. There were lots of analogies. Some guests even wondered out loud if there was a connection between the architecture and the fact that the social reception on opening day was held in the department of psychiatry. The huge building was out of sync with the other architecture on the campus. Its visual dominance of the west-end neighbourhood made some observers think of an industrial zone. At the same time, it stood dramatically between the main campus, with its well-planned green spaces, and the unplanned urban sprawl of Main Street West. No one, whatever the judgment on the architecture or the location, could argue against the contribution of such a first-class clinical, educational, and research facility to McMaster and to Hamilton.

Premier Bill Davis and a host of other dignitaries attended the ceremony. Thode made a typically humble speech, but his listeners well knew that without him they would not have been there that day. Only one regret marred the festivities: John Evans was leaving McMaster to take up the presidency of the University of Toronto, the institution that in many matters had long been McMaster's rival.

Harry Thode retired on June 30, 1972, and Arthur Bourns was named his successor. Thode now was free to turn his full attention to his research, which he did enthusiastically.

*Harry Thode (right) with (left to right) John Evans and Premier William Davis at the opening of the McMaster University Health Sciences Centre (May 1972)*

# Conclusion

Harry Thode lived for a quarter of a century after leaving the presidency. For most of that time he was active in research and went daily to his office in the Reactor Building. Even a serious setback seemed only to intensify his research absorption. In 1983 his brilliant associate Ted Rees, with whom he had published 21 papers since 1965, died suddenly. Thode took on more research than ever: "He would work late at night," recalls Sadie, "and he would skip meals. He didn't care when he ate or slept, so long as he got his research done."

Thode enjoyed good health into his early eighties and continued his long-standing habit of combining a somewhat sedentary academic life with the hard physical work of a farmer. When he was 80, on his farm in Lynden, he hauled bales of hay and on one day took in six loads. Throughout his life, he had been physically active and was especially fond of swimming and water polo, including taking an interest at one stage in his son Pat's development in both sports. With his three boys, he had gone to Hamilton and McMaster football games. For years, he followed Canadian and U.S. sports teams. These athletic interests, and a naturally strong constitution, probably helped ensure his longevity and good health. For decades, in any case, they had stood him in good stead as a counterbalance to the rigorous professional demands of scientific and administrative work. Thode was also seriously involved in music. He played the flute and the piccolo and, over the years, attended numerous concerts and recitals. Until late in his life, he maintained, as well, lively civic interests and made contributions to both non-academic and academic institutions.

Thode's father and paternal grandfather had been businessmen farmers. During his early days at McMaster, Thode had met many people in business from Hamilton and throughout Canada, thus establishing a set of relationships, some of which extended until relatively late in his life. From time to time he had been asked to give advice on technical issues. During the 1960s and 1970s, he was invited to participate financially in startup activities in several new private companies; he did invest minor amounts of money in a small number of these. As an investor he was conservative and selective, often depending on his businessman son Pat for advice. Along with Pat and his chemistry department colleague and long-time friend Dick Tomlinson, he was an original investor in the successful company now known as Gennum Corporation. Although Thode was a director of several private and public companies, including, for 17 years, the Steel Company of Canada, and had a family background in business, he was not in a major way a business person. When it was important for him to understand a particular issue, he did so, and he enjoyed the associations, but his overriding interests and development were scientific. His eminence as a scientist and academic, however, and his support of business people, gave them moral support and, sometimes, confidence in their enterprises. Thode's approach to business was a quiet, unassuming one, and he was admired and respected by those who worked with him in that context.

As the post-presidential years passed, Thode felt increasingly divorced from the day-to-day running of the university. This is probably inevitable for any individual who has been massively involved in a complex enterprise and then has no leadership role in the ongoing process. Thode was a man of exceptional academic qualities, but still he knew that he had been lucky, in the postwar years, to be principal of Hamilton College and then president of McMaster. Public and governmental support of universities was based, in Thode's time as president, on social and economic optimism, and it was generous, to the point that many academics later have looked back on the fifteen or so years from the late fifties until the early seventies as the height of the golden age of Canadian academia. The large public expenditure (and, to a much lesser extent, the private ones) that had been involved in the establishment at McMaster of a major scientific centre, with strong faculties of science, engineering, and health sciences, were not available in the succeding decades. Moreover, Thode's presidential support of widespread excellence in research and education in many of the arts disciplines had seemed to him, during most of his years as president, to be desirable and possible, without damage to his favoured scientific enterprises. He had facilitated this broad, but still selective, arts growth at McMaster in substantial ways. In 1972, however, the year of his departure from the presidency, the minister of universities, John White, announced that from then on in Ontario there was to be "more scholar for the dollar."As the real government dollars per student started to shrink, and continued to do so in Ontario almost every year for the rest of Thode's life, and as the obtaining of research funding became more complex and competitive, Thode reasoned that McMaster should narrow its academic range in favour of the sciences.

The possibility that the nuclear reactor, proudly established by Thode and opened in 1958, might be closed down was impossible for Thode to accept. He was not willing to take into account that the reactor no longer was extensively used by academic researchers, and that federal funding of it had ceased. Colleagues in physics had become more interested in solid state physics than in nuclear physics. Colleagues in chemistry now were more interested in physical chemistry and inorganic and organic chemistry than in radiochemistry. As for medical applications, new technologies had supplanted much of the reactor's usefulness. It needed costly upgrading to make it scientifically useful and the long hoped-for commercial revenues were not materializing. The reactor did continue to exist, however, and in 1996, the year before Thode's death, the promise of greater earnings from the sale of radioactive pharmaceuticals led the senate and board of governors to keep in operation this historic Thode installation.

As the years passed, Thode continued to be a productive, respected, and much-admired scientist, with a strong profile nationally and internationally, in physics, geology, and chemistry. Among his most important legacies at McMaster was the spirit of interdisciplinary cooperation that he had brought to the departments and disciplines in science, engineering, and health sciences. He had helped ensure large numbers of joint appointments of scholars with associate memberships in different departments. In this he practised administratively what was central to his own work as a scientist: the ideal of interaction and inclusion reflected the enormous scope and uncommon scientific breadth of his own abilities. In November 1996, a few months before Thode died, he was the guest of honour at a symposium organized in Toronto by the Canadian Institute for Advanced Research, called "Geology Lessons for the Future." This gathering was attended by distinguished participants from Canada, Great Britain, France, the U.S., Germany, Switzerland, India, and Austria. Many of them spoke in recognition of the outstanding scientist who was being honoured.

Thode died of heart failure on March 22, 1997. He was survived by his wife and companion for many years, Sadie Thode, by his sons and daughters-in-law, and by his grandchildren. At the memorial service in Convocation Hall there were strong tributes to the scientist, the academic builder, and the private man. One of these tributes captured particularly well the essence of Harry Thode. His grandson Steven Thode recalled visits to one of his grandfather's favourite places, the farm in Lynden: "We all remember Grandpa and Grandma when we would first arrive. Grandma was usually working in the garden. Grandpa was usually filthy, covered with tractor grease and his shirt was untucked . . . . Grandpa loved to work, and we saw that he took pride in his property. He would point out simple things like how much each bale of hay weighed, how much a tree had grown, that we could eat those berries on the neighbour's property, or how one part of his farm was higher than any piece of land around." Thode did not boast to his grandchildren about any of his accomplishments: "What we did know about Grandpa's heroics, we learned from other people."

*Mowing hay at Lynden, Ontario farm (1978)*

*Harry and Sadie Thode (1987) at home on the Lynden, Ontario farm where they lived from 1972 until 1996*

*Harry Thode in the mid-1990s*

# *Appendix One*

## Dr. Henry Thode
## Achievements And Awards

### Honours:

| | |
|---|---|
| 1946 | Member of the British Empire (MBE) |
| 1967 | Inaugural Companion of the Order of Canada (CC) |
| 1984 | Honoured by Province of Saskatchewan |
| 1984 | Member of the Inaugural Induction to the Hamilton Gallery of Distinction |
| 1989 | Order of Ontario |
| 1990 | Honorary Advisor of the Chinese Academy of Geological Sciences, Beijing, China |

### Education:

| | |
|---|---|
| 1930 | B.Sc. University of Saskatchewan |
| 1932 | M.Sc. University of Saskatchewan |
| 1934 | Ph.D. University of Chicago |

### Honourary Degrees:

| | |
|---|---|
| 1955 | D.Sc. University of Toronto |
| 1958 | LL.D. University of Saskatchewan |
| 1960 | D.Sc. University of British Columbia |
| 1960 | D.Sc. Acadia University |
| 1963 | D.Sc. Laval University |
| 1964 | D.Sc. Royal Military College of Canada |
| 1966 | D.Sc. McGill University |
| 1967 | D.Sc. Queen's University |
| 1972 | D.Sc. York University |
| 1973 | D.Sc. McMaster University |
| 1983 | LL.D. University of Regina |

## Medals:

1957     The Chemical Institute of Canada Medal
1959     Tory Medal – Royal Society of Canada
1980     Arthur L. Day Medal – Geological Society of America
1982     Centenary Medal – Royal Society of Canada
1989     The Sir William Dawson Medal – Royal Society of Canada
1993     The Montreal Medal – Chemical Institute of Canada

## Fellowships:

1943     Fellow of the Royal Society of Canada
1948     Fellow of the Chemical Institute of Canada
1954     Fellow of the Royal Society (London)
1970     Senior Foreign Scientist Fellowship awarded by the
         National Science Foundation, U.S.A.
1972     Honourary Fellow of the Chemical Institute of Canada
1974     Honourary Shell Fellow
1980     Fellow of the Geological Society of America
1981     Fellow of the American Association for the
         Advancement of Science

## Activities:

1948 & for     National Research Council of Canada
many years      Board of Directors

1948-68       Hamilton Health Association
           Board of Directors

1949-60       Royal Society of Canada President and other Positions

1950-52       Chemical Institute of Canada
           President and Vice-President

1951-81       Atomic Energy Canada
           Director and Consultant

1952 & for     St. Joseph's Hospital
many years      Member of Advisory Medical Board

1955-61       Hamilton Sanatorium
           Board of Directors

1955-61     Defence Research Board
                Board of Directors

1955-82     Ontario Research Foundation
                Board of Governors

1961-72     The Royal Botanical Gardens
                Board of Directors

1963-80     International Union of Pure and Applied Chemistry
                Member, Commission on Atomic Weights
                Member, Canadian National Committee

1965-91     Earth & Planetary Science Letters
                Member of Editorial Advisory Board

1965-73     Western New York Nuclear Research Centre, Inc.
                Board of Trustees

1966-70     The Centennial Centre of Science and Technology (Toronto)
                Board of Directors

1967-73     Brookhaven National Laboratories
                Consultant

1969-85     Stelco Inc.
                Board of Directors

1970-72     Committee of Presidents of Universities of Ontario
                Vice-Chairman

1977        Sherman Fairchild Distinguished Scholar

1980-96     Corporation of Chedoke-McMaster Hospitals
                Member

Over many   Director many private businesses
years           Member of several local clubs

## Career History:

| | |
|---|---|
| 1935-36 | Instructor in Chemistry, Pennsylvania College for Women, Pittsburgh, Pa. |
| 1936-38 | Postdoctoral Research Associate, Columbia University, New York, N.Y., with Dr. H.C. Urey |
| 1938-39 | Research Chemist, Research Laboratories, U.S. Rubber Company, Passaic, N.J. |
| 1939-42 | Assistant Professor, Dept. of Chemistry, McMaster University, Hamilton, Ontario |
| 1942-44 | Associate Professor, Dept. of Chemistry, McMaster University, Hamilton, Ontario |
| 1943-46 | National Research Council, War Research, Atomic Energy (on leave of absence from McMaster University but work was carried out at McMaster University). |
| 1944-79 | Professor, Dept. of Chemistry, McMaster University, Hamilton, Ontario |
| 1947-61 | Director of Research, McMaster University, Hamilton, Ontario |
| 1948-52 | Head, Dept. of Chemistry, McMaster University, Hamilton, Ontario |
| 1949-63 | Principal of Hamilton College, McMaster University, Hamilton, Ontario |
| 1953-97 | Associate Member, Dept. of Physics, McMaster University, Hamilton, Ontario |
| 1957-61 | Vice-President, McMaster University, Hamilton, Ontario |
| 1961-72 | President and Vice-Chancellor, McMaster University, Hamilton, Ontario |
| 1965-95 | Associate Member, Dept. of Geology, McMaster University, Hamilton, Ontario |
| 1979-97 | Professor Emeritus, Dept. of Chemistry, McMaster University, Hamilton, Ontario |
| 1994-97 | President Emeritus, McMaster University, Hamilton, Ontario |

# *Appendix Two*

## Address to the Senate by Dr. B. A. W. Jackson Wednesday November 24, 1971

Officers and Members of the Senate, and visitors:

What I must do now, I do with an inescapable feeling of regret for the occasion that prompts it, and yet with the pleasure that anyone may take in doing something that it is an honour and a privilege to do.

The time has come, as it was bound to come, when we must acknowledge our debt of gratitude to the quiet and modest man who has been the President of this University for eleven years, and when we may express our appreciation to him for making that debt so large as to be unpayable. We can, therefore, declare a kind of moral bankruptcy, and discharge the debt simply by saying thank you.

Our appreciation is another matter: it is customary and right on an occasion like this to rehearse a man's honours and achievements. Sometimes, in preparing for these solemn recitals, the biographer is embarrassed to discover that he must go over his subject's career with a fine-tooth comb in order to trap a few fragments to exhibit and admire. Not so for this man and this moment—this farm boy from Saskatchewan has had such a time of it so far that even a wide-toothed rake dragged lightly over his working years will turn up enough honours and achievements to fill several pages, an embarrassment of riches that can only be dealt with if rigorous principles of selection are applied. Accordingly Mr. Bob Taylor chose only the highlights of Harry Thode's career to put on record in a minute of appreciation for the Board of Governors yesterday morning, and it is fitting that they should also appear in the proceedings of the Senate.

May I remind you, then, that Harry Thode came to McMaster in 1939, ten years younger than the century, intent on research and teaching, a brilliant young man to whom achievement was already an old story?

143

For that fateful year, fate had prepared him. He had been working with the Nobel Prize winner, Dr. Harold Urey, on isotopes, and he was now asked by the Government to participate in vital scientific research. Such was his contribution during the war years that he was made a Member of the Order of the British Empire. Some twenty-odd years later he became, in Canada's Centennial year, a Companion of the Order of Canada. In the intervening years he had been elected a fellow of the Royal Society of Canada, president of the Chemical Institute of Canada, a member of the American Chemical Society. He is a Fellow of the Royal Society of London, an honour not frequently bestowed on anyone from outside Great Britain. Eight Universities have given him honourary degrees; he has been awarded the Royal Society of Canada Medal, and, for distinguished service to Chemistry, the Medal of the Chemical Institute of Canada. He is at present a member of the Executive Committee of Atomic Energy of Canada Limited. His ability and reputation as a scholar have taken him to the councils of scientists across the world, and combined with his energy, imagination and patience, have enabled him to plan, promote and achieve for McMaster such acquirements as the Nuclear Reactor, the Engineering School, the College of Health Sciences, and a small piece of the moon.

It was largely as a result of his efforts and capacities that Hamilton College was established after the war to develop the sciences at McMaster, and in 1948 he became its first Principal. His interest in students and research were instrumental in establishing McMaster's first doctorate programmes, and, as it was fitting, so it was probably inevitable that the earliest of these should have been in his own discipline of Chemistry.

When McMaster became non-denominational in 1957, a development toward which he had been an important activist, he was asked by the late President George Gilmour to serve as Vice-President, a position which he retained until he was appointed President in 1961.

These are the most outstanding facts of an outstanding record that is happily not yet complete. They bespeak the quality of the scholar and the administrator, and they are the solid stuff of which presentations to The Board of Governors and the public should be made.

But many of us in this body are members of faculty, and it may be that we would ask that there be added to this record something about the man himself whom we have known as a colleague as well as a President—as a colleague even while he was the President. For it seems to me that Harry Thode has always been by nature a member of faculty—that his heart and his interest have always been with the things that faculty do, and that that is why, and how, he has managed to remain a scholar and a teacher during his years as President.

They have been difficult years for Universities, and obstreperous ones for Presidents, who at times have seemed to have been distinguished by nothing so much as by their superior vulnerability as clay-pigeons in the academic shooting galleries. What with students and faculty, governments and citizens sniping and ambushing, and launching the occasional frontal attack, the vanishing-rate of Presidents has been high, so that I think it will meet with your approval if I observe that ours has stood the course remarkably well, and that while the burden has been his, the benefit has been ours.

That there have been tensions and frictions and disagreements no one will doubt, that such things could have been avoided no one this side of blue-eyed naïveté could conceive, that Harry Thode has come through them as well as any of us, and better than most of us, no one of genial spirit will deny. That no one could ask more than that of a President seems to me inconceivable; that this University should have received that much seems to me cause for even academics to permit themselves decorous expressions of praise.

That Harry developed his own techniques for survival, there can be no doubt, but they have been those of a man of integrity and good will, and they have been used not for survival only, and not for personal advancement, but of the advancement of this University, which means for the advancement of all of us.

Although it has not been noised much abroad, it can be reasonably assumed that he has had frequent and tempting chances to go elsewhere. It is not easy to judge a man's motives, but one can pass judgment on his actions. Harry Thode's seem to demonstrate a long and valuable commitment to McMaster. That, it seems to me, ought to be written large in the record.

Happily he intends to remain with us, practicing, as a member of the faculty, his teaching and research. And therefore, I may turn endwise one of the things that the Romans were reputed to have said. Instead of ave atque vale, sir, make it vale atque ave as of June the 30th next; but since I have little Latin, and most of that badly pronounced, let me put it in a free translation —'Farewell, and welcome back.'

146

# Appendix Three

## Biographical Memoir, Royal Society (London)

HENRY GEORGE THODE, M.B.E.

10 September 1910 – 22 March 1997

Elected F.R.S. 1954

BY W.B. CLARKE*, J.H. CROCKET†, R.J. GILLESPIE‡, F.R.S.,
H.R. KROUSE¶, D.M. SHAW‡ AND H.P. SCHWARCZ‡

* Department of Physics and Astronomy, McMaster University
1280 Main Street West, Hamilton, Ontario, Canada L8S 4M1
†School of Geography and Geology, McMaster University
1280 Main Street West, Hamilton, Ontario, Canada L8S 4M1
‡Department of Chemistry, McMaster University, 1280 Main Street West,
Hamilton, Ontario, Canada L8S 4M1
¶Department of Physics and Astronomy, The University of Calgary
2500 University Drive NW, Calgary, Alberta, Canada T2N 1N4

Henry George Thode was one of Canada's most distinguished physical scientists, internationally known for his work in the fields of geochemistry and nuclear chemistry. He did much of the pioneering work on the separation and concentration of stable isotopes, and made seminal studies of the natural variations in the isotopic composition of the elements in nature, particularly sulphur. Moreover, he was the principal force behind the development of McMaster University in Hamilton, Ontario, from a small church-affiliated liberal arts college with 600 students to one of Canada's leading universities with a renowned medical school and internationally recognized science and engineering facilities.

EARLY YEARS

Henry G. Thode, known to everyone as 'Harry', was born on a farm in Dundurn, Saskatchewan, Canada, in 1910 and he retained his interest in farming throughout his life, often spending relaxing weekends on his farm. After obtaining his BSc (1930) and his MSc (1932) in chemistry at the University of Saskatchewan, he was encouraged by the Saskatchewan faculty to enroll as a PhD student at the University of Chicago. He worked on the magnetic properties of solutions of metal in liquid ammonia under the supervision of Simon Freed (1, 6)*. After completing his degree in 1934 at the age of twenty-four he taught for the 1935/36 academic year at the Pennsylvania College for Women in Pittsburgh. He did not feel that this position gave him sufficient opportunity to continue the research that he wanted to do, so he took the opportunity to introduce himself to Harold C. Urey (For.Mem.R.S. 1947) at an American Chemical Society meeting in Pittsburgh and asked whether he needed a postdoctoral associate. Urey's work on deuterium had brought him the Nobel Prize in 1934 and he was then on the faculty of Columbia University in New York City. Urey was impressed by Harry's informal application and, after checking with chemists who knew Harry, gave him the position within twenty-four hours. Thus began an association that lasted over forty years until Urey's death in 1981, although Thode only worked directly with Urey from 1935 to 1938. Urey had shown that isotopes of the lighter elements differed slightly in their chemical properties and that it should be possible to trace the separation (fractionation) of these isotopes during chemical reactions. During his stay in Urey's laboratory he did pioneering work on the design and operation of systems for the partial separation of nitrogen-15 from nitrogen-14, carbon-13 from carbon-12, and sulphur-34 from sulphur-32 (2-5), beginning the work that became a dominant theme of his lifelong research. The object of the work was to obtain sufficient enrichment to allow the enriched materials to be used as isotopic tracers in such diverse fields as chemistry, biology and medicine. Urey was a scientist of ever-expanding interests, moving from physics to chemistry to biology to geology and on to astronomy and cosmology; he was clearly a role model for Thode, whose own interests expanded from physical chemistry to nuclear chemistry to geology and biology, and then to cosmochemistry.

After finishing at Columbia in 1938, Thode took a position with the US Rubber Company but after only a year he returned to Canada in 1939, surprising many people by accepting an assistant professorship in chemistry at McMaster, a small liberal arts college with only two academic buildings and 600 students. This bold and courageous step illustrates the self-confidence, independence and foresight on which his future brilliant career in science and university administration was based. This appointment gave Thode the opportunity that he wanted, namely to set up his own independent isotope laboratory. McMaster would not have seemed to many to have been the ideal place to do this and there were inevitably many problems and difficulties to overcome. But Thode was not deterred by the problems. Characteristically he simply set about solving them. The mass spectrometer had been an essential tool of Thode's research at Columbia but when he moved to McMaster there was not a single mass spectrometer in Canada and they were not available commercially. So he set out to build his own, scrounging an electromagnet and making his own spectrometer tube from Pyrex glass (8, 9). With this home-built instrument he made the first isotopic analysis of krypton and xenon from the fission of uranium-235 (10). He also set up the first isotope-fractionating column in Canada (7). It extended from the basement of the science building to the third floor in a chimney-like space that had been constructed to allow the physicists to bring light down to their basement laboratory for optics experiments. From necessity Harry became an excellent glass-blower and in later years always encouraged his students to do their own glass-blowing.

## WARTIME RESEARCH ON NUCLEAR FISSION

From 1942 to 1945 Thode was seconded to the Canadian Atomic Energy project. During this time he worked on nuclear fission and other aspects of atomic energy. This work on radioactive isotopes followed naturally from his earlier work on stable isotopes. With a group of assistants, several of whom later developed their own distinguished careers, he designed and built isotope separation equipment and mass spectrometers, and performed some brilliant pioneering work under difficult conditions. The Canadian atomic war effort was based at the University of Montreal but Harry performed much of his work at McMaster. The object of the work was to determine the nature and concentrations of the noble gases produced by the irradiation of uranium with neutrons (10). Thode was able to identify all the stable isotopes of xenon and krypton that were produced. He discovered the existence of radioactive krypton-85 and made the first measurements of its half-life. These measurements produced the first accurate information about the relative proportions of the different isotopes produced by fission, a technical and scientific contribution of great significance.

For his many scientific contributions during the war Thode was appointed a Member of the Order of the British Empire in 1946.

## STUDIES ON NUCLEAR FISSION

During the war years, security precautions prevented the publication of Thode's fission work. His first publication in this area was a 1947 paper with R.L. Graham on the design of a mass spectrometer for studies on isotopes of xenon and krypton from thermal fission of $^{235}$U (10). At the time, other researchers were astonished that such precise measurements could be made with micro (*ca.* $10^{-6}$ cc STP) amounts of xenon and krypton. Several other papers then followed (11-13, 15) that described this work in more detail and clearly showed the existence of 'fine structure' in the $^{235}$U fission yields, with unusually high yields of $^{133}$Xe and $^{134}$Xe. Later, with J. Macnamara, Thode obtained additional evidence of fine structure, which was attributed to the effects of nuclear shell structure (18, 21). Macnamara and Thode also made the first identification of xenon and krypton isotopes from the spontaneous fission of $^{238}$U (19). This work became the basis for a method for geological dating.

After 1953, Thode's work on xenon and krypton from neutron-induced and spontaneous fission in uranium continued with some work on fission yields of krypton and xenon in a range of nuclides from $^{229}$Th to $^{242}$Am. With J.A. Petruska and R.H. Tomlinson, the $^{235}$U fission yield measurements were greatly extended to cover yields of isotopes of rubidium, strontium, neodymium and samarium (27).

In 1954 Thode, with C.C. McMullen, built under contract with the Defence Research Board of Canada a high-sensitivity mass spectrometer to be used to analyse airborne debris from nuclear explosions originating in the northern USSR. This instrument was used to measure small numbers of atoms of uranium and plutonium extracted from filters carried by high-flying military aircraft over northern Canada. The isotope ratios of uranium and plutonium were used, together with isotope fission yield data, to determine the nature of the nuclear bombs.

## MCMASTER NUCLEAR REACTOR

Many of the isotope studies performed after 1959 were made possible by the existence of a nuclear reactor adjacent to the isotope research laboratory. The construction of the nuclear reactor in 1959 was itself a monument to Thode's extraordinary perseverance in the face of difficulties, and to his abilities as a scientific administrator. He and his colleagues at McMaster were able to enlist the help of E.W.R. Steacie, F.R.S., who was then head of the National Research Council of Canada. They were also able to convince the Canadian Atomic Energy establishment that first-class research with the facilities provided by a reactor could be done at a small Canadian university.

The core of the reactor and the associated equipment were designed and built in the USA, but the building was constructed by local contractors. The reactor is a 'swimming pool' type, which had been developed in the early 1950s as an intrinsically safe instrument and a versatile source of neutrons, which is well suited to university-based research applications. The construction of the reactor established McMaster as a center of nuclear research in North America and as a magnet for many young researchers and students interested in nuclear physics and chemistry, and in many other applications. It became an exceedingly useful tool for many researchers at McMaster and elsewhere.

The neutron beams that the reactor produced were used, for example, by B.N. Brockhouse (F.R.S. 1965) in his Nobel Prize-winning work on the inelastic scattering of neutrons. The neutrons have also been used in the production of radioisotopes and the study of their decay schemes, in mineral prospecting by neutron activation, and in nuclear engineering applications. Some of these studies, and indeed all those on short-lived radioisotopes, were made possible by Thode's plan to place the nuclear reactor adjacent to the isotopic research and nuclear physics laboratories. This became an advantage that few other laboratories could boast.

## KINETIC ISOTOPE EFFECTS

For many years it had been assumed that, except where isotopes of hydrogen are involved, kinetic isotope effects would be negligible or at least not susceptible to accurate measurement. In 1948 and 1949, several researchers reported surprisingly large carbon isotope effects in the electron impact and thermal decomposition of propane and malonic acid. For example, in the thermal decomposition of malonic acid labeled with $^{14}C$ in the carboxyl group the rate of rupture of a $^{12}C$-$^{12}C$ bond was found to be 12% larger than that of a $^{12}C$-$^{14}C$ bond. This result far exceeded theoretical prediction and raised the possibility that, by using a labelled compound, trace contamination had given rise to a spurious effect. Thode, with J.G. Lindsay and A.N. Bourns (22), repeated the experiment with malonic acid of natural abundance with the McMaster mass spectrometer, which was capable of measuring isotopic ratios with a precision of better than 0.1%, and observed a much smaller temperature-independent $^{12}C$/$^{13}C$ effect of just over 2%, in close agreement with the theory. Although Thode did not pursue this area of investigation, preferring to concentrate his efforts on the variation of isotopic abundances in nature, A.N. Bourns and his students followed up this work during the next several decades by applying kinetic isotope effects ($^{12}C$/$^{13}C$, $^{14}N$/$^{15}N$, $^{16}O$/$^{18}O$ and $^{32}S$/$^{34}S$) to the study of the fundamental mechanisms of the main classes of organic reactions. This important work was possible only because of the high-precision isotope-ratio mass spectrometers available in Thode's laboratory. Later, Thode was the first to show that the difference between the $^{32}S$/$^{34}S$ ratios in sulphate and sulphide was also due to kinetic isotope effects in the bacterial reduction of sulphate to sulphide.

## SULPHUR ISOTOPE STUDIES

Somehow in the midst of all his activity on nuclear fission Thode was able to maintain and develop his research on his first love, stable isotopes; indeed, this became his major field of investigation. Almost at the same time as his former mentor Urey was relocating from Columbia to Chicago and establishing a laboratory for the study of stable isotopes in geological material, Thode was embarking on a similar path at McMaster and he began to concentrate on the variations in stable isotope ratios found in nature. The work was facilitated by the development at the same time by A.O.C. Nier at Minnesota of a mass spectrometer specifically designed to measure small differences in the abundance ratios of isotopes, by simultaneously measuring the intensities of the ion beams of both isotopes. In 1949 Thode built the first of a series of instruments of this type that enabled him to detect variations of a few tenths of a per cent in the isotopic ratio of the two abundant isotopes of sulphur, $^{32}S$ and $^{34}S$. These were used by him, his research associate J. Monster, and a series of graduate students, postdoctoral fellows, and visiting scholars, to study the variations in the isotope ratios of sulphur in a large variety of naturally occurring materials.

Mass spectrometers were a vital part of Harry Thode's work. He constructed the first in Canada and continued to construct new and modified versions not only for his own laboratory but also for other institutions, including the Alberta Research Council and the University of Toronto. More importantly, most of his students and postdoctoral fellows learned the fundamentals of construction of stable isotope mass spectrometers and sample preparations lines and subsequently many of these people constructed or extensively modified stable isotope mass spectrometers and built sample preparation lines in laboratories worldwide.

Harry Thode was particularly attracted to sulphur isotope effects, which he had studied earlier at Columbia, not only because they were not being studied by Urey's group, or by anyone else, but because sulphur has multiple isotopes that span a wide range of masses: 32, 33, 34 and 36. Using advances in mass spectrometry and analytical chemistry, many of which originated in its laboratory, the McMaster group laid the foundation for a thorough understanding of isotopic fractionation observed in the laboratory and for the interpretation of sulphur isotope composition as observed in nature. Thode and his group were the first to investigate sulphur isotope geochemistry. They found that, almost everywhere they looked, sulphides were depleted in $^{34}S$ and sulphates were enriched in this isotope. This is consistent with the predictions of equilibrium thermodynamics. However, Thode quickly realized that the wide range in the isotopic composition of terrestrial sulphur was the consequence of kinetic isotope effects, in particular those associated with the low-temperature bacterial reduction of sulphate, even though it had been previously believed that such kinetic effects would be too small to be of any significance. Importantly, the isotopic evidence provided irrefutable proof that many large sulphide deposits throughout the world resulted from the bacterial reduction of sulphate. This immensely important work, performed in the immediate postwar period, was published in three landmark papers: 'Natural variations in the isotopic content of sulphur and their significance' in 1949 (16), 'The distribution of $S^{34}$ in nature and the sulfur cycle' in 1950 (17) and finally in 1951 a paper presented at the 1951 meeting of the American Chemical Society that fully considered the complete biogeochemical cycle of sulphur and the historical record of the isotope ratios of sulphate and sulphide backwards in time, leading to an assessment of the antiquity of sulphate-reducing bacteria (20). Through a few carefully conceived experiments he showed how unidirectional kinetic isotope shifts were generated by anaerobic bacteria in the reduction of sulphate to various reduced sulphur species. This ground-breaking paper was model for other studies of isotopic variations in the future. It began to be generally accepted that observed isotopic fractionations must be interpreted in the context of global cycles of the elements.

Continuing studies on sulphur isotope ratios were the most important part of Thode's research during the following years. He designed many chemical and bacterial laboratory isotope-fractionation experiments to improve the interpretation of the field observations; in combination with theoretical calculations, he was also able to derive information about reaction mechanisms. This multi-faceted approach set a new standard for sulphur isotope investigations. Through sulphur and carbon isotope data, Thode gave the scientific community a better appreciation of the extent and importance of natural microbial activity and its evolution. Over the years the term 'isotope biogeochemistry' evolved to describe this area of research, and Harry Thode must be considered one of its early pioneers.

## APPLICATIONS OF SULPHUR ISOTOPE STUDIES

Thode showed how his ideas on sulphur isotopic ratios could have important applications in many different areas. He showed, for example, that the deposits of sulphur characteristically associated with salt domes are systematically depleted in $^{34}S$ relative to coexisting sulphate and must therefore be of bacterial origin. In the field of petroleum geology his researches threw new light on the origin of oil and the nature of hydrocarbon source rocks (28, 29, 37). He showed that specific pools of oil could be marked and differentiated by their sulphur isotopic compositions. Another example was his pioneering research with J. Monster on the variation of sulphur isotopic composition of sea water over geological time (33, 35). They showed that little isotopic fractionation occurs in the precipitation of sulphate from the sea. Subsequent sulphur isotope measurements, on marine evaporites of known geological age, provided proof that the isotopic composition of sea water had varied in the past. These data provided constraints on geological processes such as the levels of volcanic activity and the extent of continental erosion and denuda-

153

tion in the past. Closely allied were Thode's studies on the importance of bacterial activity in the marine environment and his extensive researches on Precambrian iron formations. Using both sulphur and carbon isotopic ratios, he confirmed the crucial role of bacterial activity in the genesis of these formations. This work also had relevance to the origin of life from the standpoint of the rise of sulphur-reducing bacteria.

Thode also invented many other applications of his sulphur isotope studies. His work provided new constraints on the source regions of igneous rocks such as granites, and in several examples he showed the powerful diagnostic potential of sulphur isotopes in the field of ore genesis. We have already mentioned his studies of the Precambrian iron formations of the Canadian shield and elsewhere. Although these deposits are of great antiquity, Thode realized that they represented chemical sediments deposited in tectonically stable environments in which the preservation of original isotopic composition would be optimized. These iron formations, some of which were dated as being roughly 2.7 billion years old, recorded the unmistakable characteristics of sulphur isotope distributions arising from sulphur reduction by bacteria and therefore attested to the presence of these organisms in marine sediments of this age. In subsequent work on even older sedimentary rocks from Isua, West Greenland (about 3.7 billion years old), comparable sulphur isotope signatures were absent, thereby placing an upper limit on the time at which sulphur-reducing bacteria appeared in the geological record (45).

In more recent times, Harry Thode demonstrated the utility of sulphur isotopes for environmental geochemistry. A series of his papers between 1985 and 1990 were focused on core profiles of sulphur isotopic compositions from lake sediments; in these papers he showed the great utility of the sulphur isotopic composition as a monitor of anthropogenic sulphur in the environment and its relevance to environmental problems caused by acid precipitations (50-52).

## STUDIES OF METEORITIC AND LUNAR MATERIALS

Thode extended his sulphur isotope work to extraterrestrial materials, beginning with meteorites and then moving on to the study of lunar material recovered in the Apollo space programme. Thode showed that meteorites have a remarkably uniform sulphur isotopic composition, indicative of unfractionated and presumably primitive Solar System sulphur (32, 34, 44). Nevertheless, extremely small variations were observed, which were thought to be of nuclear origin. This question was of considerable significance with regard to the various models of nucleosynthesis. The key to identifying any sulphur produced by nuclear processes lay in the determination of the rarer isotopes of sulphur, namely $^{33}$S and $^{36}$S (the latter representing about 1 part in

7000 of meteoritic sulphur). New analytical procedures were developed to permit the determination of these isotopes with sufficient sensitivity and accuracy, and it was established that there was no evidence in meteorites for a variation in sulphur isotopic abundances due to inhomogeneities in the processes of nucleosynthesis. These studies not only contributed significantly to the understanding of the origin of meteorites but laid much of the analytical groundwork for Thode's participation in the study of lunar rocks. McMaster was one of the few Canadian universities to be involved in the study of the famous 'moon rocks'. Much of this effort in lunar studies was carried out in the 1970s in collaboration with C.E. Rees and was focused mainly on lunar soil (regolith). They obtained the first sulphur isotope data on lunar materials by using the rare $^{36}$S and $^{33}$S isotopes (38-43, 36-49). This work helped to confirm the large difference in isotopic composition between lunar rocks and soils, and was especially important in documenting the very complex history of the lunar regolith.

Throughout Harry's long career, his laboratory generated a steady flow of high-quality data bearing on fundamental aspects of sulphur isotope chemistry. His contributions to the quantitative foundation of sulphur isotope geochemistry were outstanding, and he showed an amazing insight into how these data could be used in practical applications, especially in the Earth sciences. He is quite properly regarded as the father of sulphur isotope geochemistry. It was mainly for this work that he was awarded the Arthur L. Day Medal of the Geological Society of America in 1980.

## OTHER ISOTOPE STUDIES

Thode also worked on isotopes of elements other than sulphur, carbon, nitrogen and oxygen. With J. Macnamara, F.P. Lossing and C.B. Collins he was the first to show that the isotopic composition of terrestrial boron was variable (14). They encountered considerable experimental difficulties in this work and perhaps for this reason there was much controversy in the open literature concerning the existence of $^{10}$B/$^{11}$B variations during the next ten years. In 1961, because of the controversy and for other reasons, Thode, with C.C. McMullen and C.B. Cragg, repeated the $^{10}$B/$^{11}$B ratio work with improved methods (30). They showed that the previous absolute ratios were slightly high but the isotopic variation was essentially correct. In recent years, further developments in analytical techniques have enabled other researchers to exploit the relatively large variations in boron isotope ratio as powerful tracers for geochemical processes.

Thode's work on sulphur isotopes prompted him to look for similar effects in selenium. With his student H.R. Krouse, he conducted a study of $^{76}$Se/$^{82}$Se ratios and found variations of up to 1.5%, with plant materials and soil showing the largest variations on either side of the meteoritic value (31). In laboratory experiments, a kinetic isotope effect of 1.5% was found in the reduction of selenite to elemental selenium. Thode and his student C.E. Rees subsequently extended the observations (36) and these terrestrial selenium isotope variations are now beginning to be exploited as tracers by geochemists.

## RADIOIODINE STUDIES

Thode was intensely interested in all aspects of isotope chemistry. In 1949 he was instrumental in the formation of a clinical research laboratory at McMaster University in which he and his colleagues conducted research on the use of radioiodine ($^{131}$I) in the diagnosis and treatment of thyroid function disorders (23). Although the use of $^{131}$I in the diagnosis and treatment of thyroid disorders was fairly widespread at the time, Thode and his co-workers M.W. Johns, J.H. Gregson, G.C. Foster and C.H. Jaimet made significant improvements in the sensitivity of $^{131}$I detection. Thode also made further studies in this area (24-26). The test that he and his collaborators developed for the diagnosis of thyroid function disorders is still considered to be the most reliable.

Thode's radioiodine group was unusually effective because chemists, physicists and medical people were operating as a team. Thode greatly enjoyed this type of cooperative interdisciplinary work and he became a lifelong promoter of interdisciplinary research. Although the radioiodine work occupied only a brief period in his long career, it might indeed have set the stage for the creation of the McMaster University Medical Centre in 1965.

## ADMINISTRATION

Thode's wartime work on fission products and related nuclear topics led him into many governmental and other national advisory scientific bodies, and inevitably he became increasingly involved in administrative tasks both inside and outside the university. In 1959 he was part of a National Research Council of Canada delegation invited by the Soviet Academy of Sciences to visit the Soviet Union, which led to an agreement for the exchange of scientists between Canada and the Soviet Union. From 1963 to 1979 he was a member of the commission on Atomic Weights of the Inorganic Chemistry Division of IUPAC. Over the years many members of the commission were former students or postdoctoral fellows of Harry Thode's.

Other important positions that he held included his being a member of the National Research Council of Canada, a member of the Board of Governors of the Ontario Research Foundation, and a Director and member of the

Executive Committee of Atomic Energy of Canada Limited. In 1954 he was President of the Royal Society of Canada. In 1951-52 he was Vice-President and President of the Chemical Institute of Canada. From 1961-1972 he was a member of the Board of Directors of the Royal Botanical Gardens in Hamilton, Ontario. From 1970 to 1972 he was Vice-Chairman of the Committee of Presidents of the Universities of Ontario.

At McMaster his involvement with the administration of the university increased rapidly. Having been appointed Assistant Professor in 1939, he was already a full professor by 1944, becoming Director of Research for the university in 1947 and Head of the Chemistry Department in 1948. In 1949 he became Principal of Hamilton College (a new entity designed to give some fiscal independence from the university's church affiliation). Then, when the university severed its church affiliation, he became successively Vice-President of the university from 1957 to 1961 and then from 1961 to 1972 President of the university. He retired in 1972 to become Professor Emeritus in the Department of Chemistry. However, he never really retired, continuing his research activities and coming on campus to his office almost every day up to his death.

In 1989 his colleagues celebrated a remarkable and unique anniversary with him, namely a record of fifty years of continuous research support from the National Research Council of Canada (later the Natural Sciences and Engineering Research Council). Under his leadership the university went from strength to strength and today it is one of Canada's leading universities. He created the new Faculty of Engineering in 1957 and appointed talented young faculty members to provide a flying start. The creation of a first-class medical research centre at McMaster had long been one of Thode's dreams and this became a reality with the opening of a building in 1965 for the new College of Health Sciences, comprising a health sciences centre and a hospital. Again, the appointment of talented young faculty members soon enabled the McMaster medical school to achieve an international reputation, particularly for its innovative teaching methods. Indeed, Thode had an uncanny ability to pick the right people for the job. He appointed many young professors whose subsequent outstanding work contributed greatly to the enhancement of the reputation of McMaster University. His firm and persuasive leadership was of immeasurable benefit to the university. His enthusiasm, self-confidence and optimism enabled him to overcome many obstacles and inspired his colleagues to follow and support his farsighted vision for the university. Throughout his career, Harry Thode received many awards and honours recognizing his work. He was elected a fellow of the Royal Society of Canada in 1943 at the young age of thirty-three, and a Fellow of The Royal Society in 1954. He was awarded the Arthur L. Day Medal of the Geological Society of America in 1980, and he received the Tory, Centenary and Dawson

Medals of the Royal Society of Canada. He received honorary degrees from many Canadian universities and in 1967 he was the first chemist to be named Companion of the Order of Canada, the highest honour that Canada awards to its most distinguished citizens.

Harry Thode will be remembered as a man who loved science, did superb scientific work and was an extraordinarily effective administrator. He had vision, contagious enthusiasm, amazing persuasiveness, and resolute determination. He was always modest about his achievements and gave his time generously to his friends and colleagues. Harry was blessed with a very happy family life: Sadie, his wife of sixty-two years, cheerful, outgoing, hospitable, was the perfect partner and gave him essential and constant support in all his scientific and administrative activities. He is survived by Sadie, his three sons, John Charles, Henry Patrick, and Richard Lee, and eight grandchildren.

*Harry working on an isotope separation column with his graduate students J. Zeigler and F.O. Walkling (right), in 1940*

*Harry Thode (left) with his elder brother Eckart, in about 1915*

*Harry in the McMaster mass spectrometer laboratory, in 1949*

*Harry examining a model of a nuclear reactor with W.H. Fleming (left)
and D.M. Hedden, in 1956*

# *Bibliography*

The following publications are those referred to directly in the text. A full bibliography appears on the accompanying microfiche, numbered as in the second column. A photocopy is available from The Royal Society's Library at cost.

(1)   (2)   1934   (With S. Freed) A magnetic study of the metallic state and the Fermi-Dirac statistics. *Nature* **134**, 774.

(2)   (4)   1937   (With H.C. Urey, M. Fox & J.R. Huffman) A concentration of $N^{15}$ by a chemical exchange reaction. *J. Am. Chem. Soc.* **59**, 1407.

(3)   (5)       (With H.C. Urey, J.F. Huffman & M. Fox) Concentration of $N^{15}$ by chemical methods. *J. Chem. Phys.* **5**, 856-868.

(4)   (6)   1938   (With J.E. Gorham & H.C. Urey) The concentration of $N^{15}$ and $S^{34}$. *J. Chem. Phys.* **6**, 296.

(5)   (7)   1939   (With H.C. Urey) The further concentration of $N^{15}$. *J. Chem. Phys.* **7**, 34-39.

(6)   (8)       (With S. Freed) On the nature of the solutions of metallic sodium in liquid ammonia. *J. Chem. Phys.* **7**, 85-86.

(7)   (12)   1942   (With F.O. Walkling) Column packing and the separation of isotopes. *Can. J. Res.* B **20**, 61-68.

(8)   (13)   1943   Mass spectrometry. The mass spectrometer and some uses of stable isotopes in chemistry. *Can. Chem. Process Ind.* **27**, 647-650.

(9)   (16)   1945   (With R.L. Graham & J.A. Ziegler) A mass spectrometer and the measurement of isotope exchange factors. *Can. J. Res.* B **23**, 40-47.

(10)   (18)   1947   (With R.L. Graham) A mass spectrometer investigation of the isotopes of xenon and krypton resulting from the fission of $U^{235}$ by thermal neutrons. *Can. J. Res.* A **25**, 1-14.

(11)   (22)       (With R.L. Graham & A.L. Harkness) An a.c. operated mass spectrometer for isotope abundance measurements. *J. Scient. Instrum.* **24**, 119-128.

(12)   (23)       (With R.L. Graham) Isotope abundance measurements. In *Proc. XIth International Congress of Pure and Applied Chemistry, London*, 17-24 July, pp. 627-636.

(13) (25)      (With M. Loundsbury & S. Epstein) The isotopic composition of normal krypton and xenon. *Phys. Rev.* **72**, 517-518.

(14) (27) 1948  (With J. Macnamara, F.P. Lossing & C.B. Collins) Natural variations in the isotopic content of boron and its chemical atomic weight. *J. Am. Chem. Soc.* **70**, 3001-3008.

(15) (28)      Mass spectrometry and nuclear chemistry. *Nucleonics* **3**, 14-24.

(16) (31) 1949  (With J. Macnamara & C.B. Collins) Natural variations in the isotopic content of sulphur and their significance. *Can. J. Res.* B **27**, 361-373.

(17) (34) 1950  (With A. Szabo, A. Tudge & J. Macnamara) The distribution of $S^{34}$ in nature and the sulfur cycle. *Science* **111**, 464-465.

(18) (35)      (With J. Macnamara & C.B. Collins) The fission yield of $Xe^{133}$ and fine structure in the mass yield curve. *Phys. Rev.* **78**, 129-134.

(19) (40)      (With J. Macnamara) The isotopes of xenon and krypton in pitchblende and the spontaneous fission of $U^{238}$. *Phys. Rev.* **80**, 471-472.

(20) (42) 1951  (With J. Macnamara) The distribution of $S^{34}$ in nature and the origin of native sulfur deposits. *Research* **4**, 582.

(21) (43)      Fission product yields and shell structure in atomic nuclei. *Trans. R. Soc. Can.* **45**, 1-17.

(22) (44)      (With J.G. Lindsay & A.N. Bourns) $C^{13}$ isotope effect in the decarboxylation of normal malonic acid. *Can. J. Chem.* **29**, 192-200.

(23) (50) 1953  (With M.W. Johns, J.H. Gregson, G.C. Foster & C.H. Jaimet) Radioiodine 131 in the diagnosis of thyroid function. *Can. Med. Ass. J.* **68**, 132-137.

(24) (62) 1954  (With C.H. Jaimet and S. Kirkwood) Studies and diagnostic tests of thyroid and salivary gland function with radioiodine. *New Engl. J. Med.* **251**, 129-134.

(25) (63)      (With C.H. Jaimet and S. Kirkwood) Studies and diagnostic tests of salivary and thyroid gland function with radioiodine. In *Proceedings of the 2nd Radioisotope Conference, Oxford, July* (ed. J.E. Johnston), pp. 55-67. London: Butterworths Scientific Publications.

(26) (65) 1955  (With C.H. Jaimet) Thyroid function studies on children receiving cobalt therapy. *J. Am. Med. Ass.* **158**. 1353-1355.

(27) (68)      (With J.A. Petruska & R.H. Tomlinson) The absolute fission yields of twenty-eight mass chains in the thermal neutron fission of $U^{235}$. *Can. J. Phys.* **33**, 693-706.

(28)  (80)  1958  (With J. Monster & H.B. Dunford) Sulphur isotope abundances in petroleum and associated materials. *Bull. Am. Ass. Petrol. Geol.* **42**, 2619-2641.

(29)  (81)        (With A.G. Harrison) Sulphur isotope abundances in hydro-carbons and source rocks of Uinta Basin, Utah. *Bull. Am. Ass. Petrol. Geol.* **42**, 2642-2649.

(30)  (88)  1961  (With C.C. McMullen & C.B. Cragg) Absolute ratio of $B^{11}/B^{10}$ in Searles Lake borax. *Geochim. Cosmochim. Acta* **23**, 147-149.

(31)  (94)  1962  (With H.R. Krouse) Thermodynamic properties and geochemistry of isotopic compounds of selenium. *Can. J. Chem.* **40**, 367-375.

(32)  (95)  1963  (With M. Shima & W.H. Gross) Sulfur isotope abundances in basic sills, differentiated granites and meteorites. *J. Geophys. Res.* **68**, 2835-2847.

(33)  (99)  1964  (With J. Monster) The sulphur isotope abundances in evaporites and in ancient oceans. In *Vernadsky memorial, vol.* 2, pp. 589-600. Moscow. [in Russian.] [English translation in *Chemistry of the Earth's crust*, vol. 2, pp. 630-641. Jerusalem: Israel Program for Scientific Translation.]

(34)  (108) 1965  (With J. Monster & E. Anders) $^{34}S/^{32}S$ ratios for the different forms of sulphur in the Orgueil meteorite and their mode of formation. *Geochim. Cosmochim. Acta* **29**, 773-779.

(35)  (112)       (With J. Monster) Sulfur-isotope geochemistry of petroleum, evaporites and ancient seas. In *Fluids in subsurface environments – a symposium* (American Association of Petroleum Geologists Memoir 4), pp. 367-377.

(36)  (113) 1966  (With C.E. Rees) Selenium isotope effects in the reduction of sodium selenite and of sodium selenate. *Can. J. Chem.* **44**, 419-427.

(37)  (122) 1970  (With J. Monster) Sulfur isotope abundances and genetic relations of oil accumulations in the Middle East Basin. *Bull. Am. Ass. Petrol. Geol.* **54**, 627-637.

(38)  (129) 1971  (with C.E. Rees) Measurement of sulphur concentrations and the isotope ratios $^{33}S/^{32}S$, $^{34}S/^{32}S$ and $^{36}S/^{32}S$ in Apollo 12 samples. *Earth Planet. Sci. Lett.* **12**, 434-438.

(39)  (132) 1972  (with C.E. Rees) Sulphur contents and isotope ratios in lunar samples. In *Lunar Science III* (ed. C. Watkins), pp. 749-751. Houston, Texas: Lunar Science Institute.

(40)  (133)       (With C.E. Rees) Sulphur concentrations and isotope ratios in Apollo 14 and 15 samples. In *The Apollo 15 lunar samples* (ed. J.W. Chamberlain & C. Watkins), pp. 402-403. Houston, Texas: Lunar Science Institute.

(41) (134)        (With C.E. Rees) Sulphur concentrations and isotope ratios in lunar samples. In *Proc. Third Lunar Sci. Conf. (Geochim. Cosmochim. Acta* suppl. 3), vol. 2, pp. 1479-1485.

(42) (137) 1974   (With C.E. Rees) Sulphur concentrations and isotope ratios in Apollo 16 and 17 samples. In *Proc. Fifth Lunar Sci. Conf. (Geochim. Cosmochim. Acta* suppl. 5), pp. 1963-1973.

(43) (141) 1976   (With C.E. Rees) Sulphur isotopes in grain size fractions of lunar soils. In *Proc. Seventh Lunar Sci. Conf. (Geochim. Cosmochim. Acta* suppl. 7), pp. 459-468.

(44) (143) 1977   (With C.E. Rees) A $^{33}$S anomaly in the Allende meteorite. *Geochim. Cosmochim. Acta* **41**, 1679-1682.

(45) (146) 1979   (With J. Monster, P.W.U. Appel, M. Schidlowski, C.M. Carmichael & D. Bridgewater) Sulfur isotope studies in Early Archean sediments from Isua, West Greenland: implications for the antiquity of bacterial sulfate reduction. *Geochim. Cosmochim. Acta* **43**, 405-413.

(46) (148)        (With C.E. Rees) Sulphur isotopes in lunar and meteorite samples. In *Proc. Tenth Lunar Sci. Conf. (Geochim. Cosmochim. Acta* suppl. 11.), vol 2, pp. 1629-1636.

(47) (149) 1980   (With C.E. McEwing & C.E. Rees) Sulphur isotope effects in the dissociation and evaporation of troilite. A possible mechanism for $^{34}$S enrichment in lunar soils. *Geochim. Cosmochim. Acta* **44**, 565-571.

(48) (152) 1983   (With T. Ding & C.E. Rees) Sulphur content and sulphur isotope composition of orange and black glasses in Apollo 17 drive tube 74002/1. *Geochim. Cosmochim. Acta* **47**, 491-496.

(49) (154)        (With C.E. Rees) Sulphur isotopes in lunar-soils-surface vs bulk properties. In *Lunar and planetary science XIV*, pp. 634-635. Houston, Texas: Lunar and Planetary Science Institute.

(50) (160) 1985   (With M. Dickman) The rate of lake acidification in four lakes north of Lake Superior and its relationship to downcore sulphur isotope ratios. *Water Air Soil Pollut.* **26**, 233-253.

(51) (162) 1986   (With M.E. Thompson & A.S. Fraser) Sulfate yields and isotopic ratios of sulfate sulphur in rivers of the N.W.T. *J. Appl. Geochem.* **1**, 311-314.

(52) (163) 1987   (With M. Dickman & S.S. Rao) Effects of acid precipitation on sediment down core profiles of diatoms. Bacterial densities and sulphur isotope ratios in lakes north of Lake Superior. *Archiv. Hydrobiol.* suppl. **74**, 397-422.

# Appendix Four

# Biographical Memoir, Geological Society of America

**Memorial to Henry G. Thode**
**1910-1997**

DENIS M. SHAW
McMaster University, Hamilton, Ontario, Canada L8S 4M1

SAM EPSTEIN
California Institute of Technology, Pasadena, California

JOHN M. HAYES
Woods Hole Oceanographic Institution, Woods Hole, Massachusetts

Leading geochemist, nuclear chemist, former president of McMaster University, farmer, Member of the British Empire, Companion of the Order of Canada, and 1980 Arthur L. Day medallist of the Geological Society of America, Harry Thode played many diverse roles and was warmly esteemed and respected in each of them.

Many knew him not only from his service as president of McMaster University, but as the principal developer of that institution. Another group of scientists would probably identify him mainly as a nuclear physicist. People from many walks of life in Hamilton, Ontario, would think of Harry as a very successful and creative businessman and contributor to civic life.

Henry Thode completed a B.Sc. in honours chemistry at the University of Saskatchewan in 1930, stayed to complete an M.Sc. two years later, and, just two years after that, at the age of 24, completed his Ph.D. in physical chemistry at the University of Chicago. In 1934, it was difficult to find a job. Harry found one at the Pennsylvania College for Women, in Pittsburgh, and he began teaching there in 1935. In September 1936, the American Chemical Society held its national meeting in Pittsburgh, and Harry took the opportunity to talk to Harold C. Urey and ask whether he needed a postdoctoral research associate. Urey's work on deuterium, the heavy isotope of hydrogen, had brought him the Nobel prize in chemistry in 1934, and he was then on the faculty of Columbia University in New York City. Harry's informal application fit Urey's style perfectly, and it yielded a job within 24 hours, since it was easy for Urey to check promptly with chemists who had known Harry in Chicago. He said yes the next day.

Harry Thode's two-year stay in Urey's laboratories yielded seven papers dealing mostly with the design and operation of systems for the separation of nitrogen-15 from nitrogen-14, carbon-13 from carbon-12, and sulfur-34 from sulfur-32. In the hands of Urey's biochemical colleagues, the newly available separated isotopes were driving a revolution by revealing the dynamic nature of biochemistry. For example, the availability of useful quantities of nitrogen-15 led to the discovery that proteins were constantly torn apart and rebuilt rather than synthesized and then degraded only when they were no longer needed. It is almost inconceivable to us now that this was not known only 60 years ago.

During those years at Columbia, Thode thought constantly about how to achieve not total separation of one isotope from another, but at least substantial enrichment of the rare isotopes, so that the enriched material could serve as an isotopic tracer. The key was to find a reaction that led to the greatest possible isotopic fractionation in a single step and then to devise some practical means of repeating it thousands of times.

Finishing up at Columbia, Harry first took a job with U.S. Rubber Company, across the Hudson River in New Jersey, but found his way back to Canada when, in 1939, he accepted an assistant professorship in chemistry at McMaster University. It was then a small, church-affiliated liberal arts college with two buildings. The director of research at U.S. Rubber—who would have thought of Harry as the hotshot from Urey's group—could hardly believe it when he described why he was leaving. It was, however, clearly a declaration of independence that any American could appreciate: a breathtaking combination of self-confident intelligence, foresight, and personal courage.

At Columbia, mass spectrometers had been part of the landscape, but when Harry moved to McMaster there were none anywhere in Canada, and they were not commercial products. So Harry found a magnet and fabricated his own spectrometer tube from Pyrex glass, rather than the customary stainless steel. Its difficult birth notwithstanding, that mass spectrometer went on to demonstrate convincingly that the operator and the choice of problems are

168

always more important than the instrument. With it, Harry produced the first analyses of the gases resulting from the fission of uranium.

For part of the war Harry Thode was seconded to carry out war research. One of us, Sam Epstein, first encountered him at the University of Montreal, which at that time housed the Canadian atomic war effort. Harry was working in one of the small English groups whose objective was to determine the nature and concentrations of the rare gases in neutron-irradiated uranium metal. He was able to identify all of the isotopes of xenon and krypton which were produced by slow neutron uranium fission. These measurements provided wartime physicists with their first information about the relative proportions of the different isotopes produced by this fission. This was a technical and scientific contribution of huge significance and probably explains his early election to the Royal Society of Canada. When the University of Montreal laboratories closed down, this collaboration continued at McMaster University, but not for long. Thode acted in a typically unselfish manner and recommended that Epstein accept an offer to go to a job with Harold Urey at the University of Chicago.

When the dust of war settled, Harry had (1) the knowledge of processes of isotopic fractionation that he had gained in Urey's lab, (2) a view from that same era of biology and biochemistry at their best, and (3) the mass spectroscopic and analytical capabilities that he had developed at Hamilton. In the late 1930s, Al Nier had shown that the ratio of carbon-13 to carbon-12 varied among materials at Earth's surface, and evidence was accumulating that distributions of the isotopes of other elements were wildly uneven. The isotopic variations were tiny in absolute terms: 1.112% carbon-13 in a limestone and 1.087% carbon-13 in some organic material. Measuring them was an interesting challenge. At that stage even the founding fathers of isotopic geochemistry were publishing accounts of exploration rather than explanation.

Harry, on the other hand, was able to look at these natural fractionations and to know exactly what sort of processes might be causing them. While others explored, Harry explored and explained. He knew that Urey's new research group at Chicago was aggressively examining variations in the abundances of the isotopes of carbon and oxygen. Those in oxygen were viewed as particularly interesting because they seemed to be controlled by temperature, and that was something that could be understood by a physicist. No one seemed to be tackling sulphur, probably because its chemistry is so notoriously complex. Harry was attracted to it not only because it was unclaimed but because it had multiple isotopes that spanned a wide range of masses–32, 33, 34, and 36. It turned out that the fractionations were huge. Almost everywhere the McMaster group looked, sulfides were depleted in sulphur-34 and sulfates were enriched. Thode immediately identified these findings as an isotopic fractionation associated with the action of sulfate-reducing bacteria. That insight stimulated the research that has led to our present recognition that fully half of the organic material reaching the seafloor is oxidized at the expense of sulfate rather than $O_2$. A paper presented in 1951 at a meeting of the American Chemical Society had it all: a systematic consideration of the complete biogeochemical cycle of sulphur—its oxidation and reduction, erosion, burial, and volcanic emanations. This sort of thing showed up much later in papers from other groups—and a historical record of the isotope ratios of sulfate and sulfide backward in time, leading to an assessment of the antiquity of sulfate-reducing bacteria. Subsequent papers showed that the deposits of elemental sulphur that are so prominently associated with salt domes are systematically depleted relative to coexisting sulfate and must be of bacterial origin.

The titles of these papers are distinctive because they deal with what's going on as well as what's there. The first, in 1949, was "Natural variations in the isotopic content of sulphur *and their significance*." A 1950 paper in Nature was entitled "The distribution of sulphur-34 in nature and the *sulphur cycle*." These papers introduced what we would now call a "process orientation." They provided new information about how nature works, and they were recognized. Now everyone realizes that observed fractionations must be seen in the context of the global cycles of the elements.

Harry's wartime work on fission products and related nuclear topics led Harry Thode into many governmental and other national advisory scientific bodies, and attracted a growing group of students and colleagues at McMaster. Inevitably, although probably not by design, he became increasingly involved in administrative tasks. He nevertheless found time to interest himself in the projects of young colleagues, such as another one of us, Denis Shaw. His subsequent support in many ways really determined why many of us stayed at McMaster and turned down offers elsewhere. We never collaborated directly on any research project, but he would often come over to discuss what he was doing and to try to understand the strange reasoning of geologists.

These discussions continued even after he became heavily involved in administrative tasks, beginning in 1949 when he became principal of Hamilton College (a new entity, designed for some fiscal independence from the university's church affiliations) and continuing later as vice-president and then, from 1961 to 1972, as president of the university. Throughout that period, he was able to keep Saturdays free for science. It was in this period also that his work became more devoted to cosmochemical and medical topics, interests that continued to the end of his life. In the latter field he spearheaded several innovations in the application of radioisotopes as diagnostic tools.

One of Harry Thode's major achievements was to persuade the atomic energy authorities that there was a need in Canada for a nuclear reactor devoted to research for industry and academia, and to install such as facility at his home institution. The McMaster Nuclear Reactor has been in operation almost continuously since 1959.

This interest in applied science led Thode into several innovative enterprises. One of the most successful has been a local integrated circuit company, whose inauguration owed much to his encouragement and help.

He has received the Tory, Centenary, and Dawson Medals of the Royal Society of Canada, which he served as president in 1959. In 1980 he was the Arthur L. Day medallist of the Geological Society of America, an award that places him in the company of the most famous chemists and physicists that have contributed to the geological sciences. He was named a Fellow of the Royal Society of Canada in 1943, when he was 33 years old, and a Fellow of the Royal Society of London just 11 years later.

Although officially retired many years ago, he continued an active scientific career, going to his office on campus most days of the week, almost until his death in 1997. This was a man who was unselfish, loved science, and contributed enormously to the lives of many people.